GEO-WHIZ!

By Susan Mondshein Tejada

Art by Laurie Hamilton

Gee-whiz, it's the Corkscrew! That's what people have nicknamed this passageway in Antelope Canyon, in Arizona. Over millions of years, streams have carved and polished its swirling walls of reddish sandstone, making them shiny and slick. Your journey into geography starts beyond these walls. Just turn the page.

© GALEN ROWELL—PETER ARNOLD, INC.

■ BOOKS FOR WORLD EXPLORERS
■ NATIONAL GEOGRAPHIC SOCIETY

CONTENTS

ANTHONY BANNISTER

GORDON GAHAN

▲ They're off! Gemsbok
(GEMZ-bahk) race across
the Namib (NAHM-ib)
Desert, in Africa. A kind of
antelope, the gemsbok uses
its powerful legs to run
from predators. If cornered,
it will fight with its horns.
◀ It's a long haul up
Haleakala (holl-ee-ahk-uh-
LAH) Crater. The volcano,
on the Hawaiian island of
Maui (MOHW-ee), rises
10,023 feet. Its name

INTRODUCTION

Ready, set, read! By the time you finish this book, you'll be a certified geo-whiz. What's a geo-whiz? That's someone who knows a lot about geography. Geography is the study of the earth and of every creature on it. Each chapter in the book will introduce you to an element of geography. You'll take a look at land features and water features. You'll meet animals and plants that thrive, or live well, only in certain climates. You'll find out how people around the world live and celebrate. A map at the beginning of each chapter will show you where on earth to find features and creatures in the chapter.

Every few pages, you'll come across a "Geo-Quiz!" Each time, you can quiz yourself and your friends on far-out geography facts. Try this: If you traveled around the earth at the Equator, how far would you go? The answer is 24,902 miles. To become a geo-whiz, you'll have to go a lot farther than that. You'll have to scale cliffs, dive into oceans, and journey from the North Pole to the South Pole. So as you pack your climbing boots, take your scuba gear and parka, too. You're on your way!

◀ *It's jam-packed. It's Buenos Aires (BWAY-nuh-SAR-eez)—the capital of Argentina, a country in South America. One-third of all Argentinians live in and around the city.*

LOREN MCINTYRE

◀ *Rice is a top crop on the Asian island of Sri Lanka (sree LAHNG-ka)—and a top food worldwide.*

ROBERT FRERCK/ODYSSEY PRODUCTIONS, CHICAGO

3

What a view! From Mount McKinley, in Alaska, a climber looks out over high-flying clouds. Peaks of other tall mountains poke through the clouds. Indians named Mount McKinley Denali, "the high one."

Looking At the Land

1

Where can you stand so that you are above the clouds, yet with your feet planted firmly on the ground? On a mountain! Try it. Join this climber on a ledge of Alaska's Mount McKinley. At 20,320 feet above sea level, McKinley is the tallest mountain in North America. From here, you'll see two other tall peaks—Mount Foraker and Mount Hunter.

If you're going to become a geo-whiz, a visit to McKinley is just the beginning. You'll want to visit other mountains around the world, too. They include a mountain that rises from the ocean floor and another mountain that formed in just five months.

On your geo-journey, you could spend a lot of time exploring only mountains. But then you'd miss seeing other land features: caves and canyons, rocks and dunes, valleys and islands. In this chapter, you'll explore them all. You'll find out that the earth is made up of land that is high, land that is low, land that is flat, and land that is shaped into cliffs. Forces within the earth continuously change the land. Outside forces sculpt different surface features.

Geologists, scientists who study the earth, call the earth's outer layer the crust. The crust is made up of huge, puzzle-like pieces called plates. The plates carry the continents, the oceans, and you. Like gigantic rafts, the plates float slowly on a sea of partly melted rock which is beneath the crust. They move between a fraction of an inch and five inches a year. Sometimes the plates crunch into each other. Sometimes a single plate cracks. Sometimes the edge of one plate dives beneath the edge of another.

With these movements, the surface of the land slowly changes. Mountains rise. Valleys sink. Volcanoes erupt. Plate movement elevates the land. Then wind, water, and ice shape the land into some of the features you'll see in this chapter. What carved the Grand Canyon, in Arizona? Water did. What fashioned dunes in deserts around the world? Wind did. To find out how, read on.

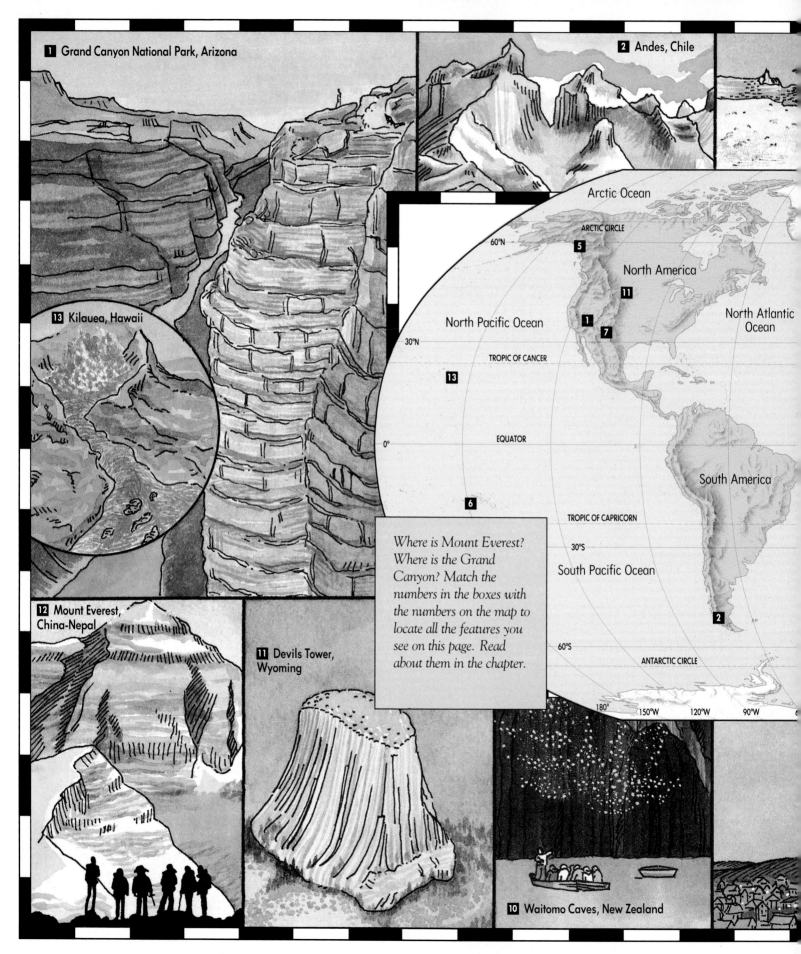

1 Grand Canyon National Park, Arizona

2 Andes, Chile

13 Kilauea, Hawaii

Arctic Ocean

ARCTIC CIRCLE

60°N

5

North America

11

North Pacific Ocean

1

North Atlantic Ocean

7

30°N

TROPIC OF CANCER

13

0° EQUATOR

South America

6

TROPIC OF CAPRICORN

30°S

South Pacific Ocean

Where is Mount Everest? Where is the Grand Canyon? Match the numbers in the boxes with the numbers on the map to locate all the features you see on this page. Read about them in the chapter.

2

60°S

ANTARCTIC CIRCLE

180° 150°W 120°W 90°W

12 Mount Everest, China-Nepal

11 Devils Tower, Wyoming

10 Waitomo Caves, New Zealand

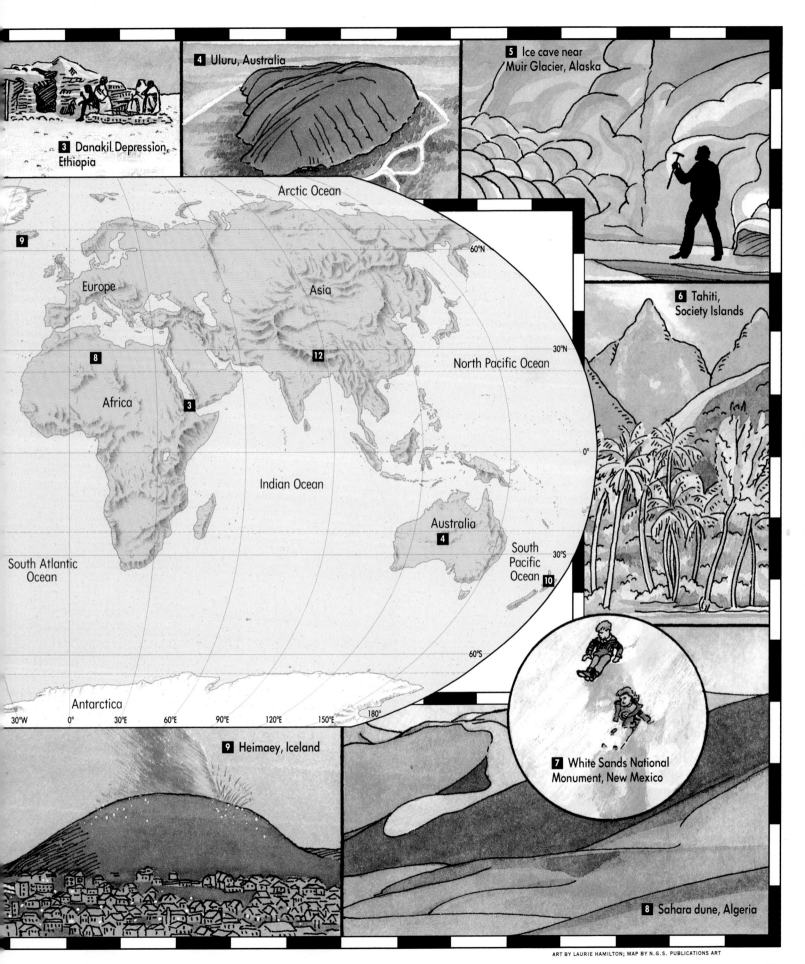

3 Danakil Depression, Ethiopia

4 Uluru, Australia

5 Ice cave near Muir Glacier, Alaska

6 Tahiti, Society Islands

Arctic Ocean

Europe

Asia

60°N

30°N

North Pacific Ocean

Africa

3

0°

Indian Ocean

Australia

4

South Atlantic Ocean

30°S

South Pacific Ocean

10

60°S

Antarctica

30°W   0°   30°E   60°E   90°E   120°E   150°E   180°

8

12

9

7 White Sands National Monument, New Mexico

9 Heimaey, Iceland

8 Sahara dune, Algeria

ART BY LAURIE HAMILTON; MAP BY N.G.S. PUBLICATIONS ART

Big Tops

ART WOLFE

Welcome to Mount Everest! It towers nearly five and a half miles into the sky. Its claim to fame: It is the tallest mountain above sea level. To look at Everest, you might think that it had been around since the beginning of time. You might think that it would stand until the end of time, too. According to scientists, neither is the case. They say that mountains have been continuously rising and wearing down for more than four billion years. Everest, which began forming some 40 to 60 million years ago, is just one example of this process.

Everest rose, along with the mountains around it, when continents on two of the earth's plates collided. Over millions of years, pressure caused the land at the edge of the continents to buckle and fold into mountains. To see how mountains fold, place two hand towels on a table and push their ends together until the towels wrinkle. Consider each wrinkle a mountain. Even as mountains form, water, ice, and wind wear them away, or erode them. After a mountain stops rising, erosion continues to wear it away. After millions of years, the mountain may disappear.

Mountains cover one-quarter of the land on earth. As you tour them, you'll see snowy mountains, grassy mountains, mountains covered with tropical vegetation, and mountains surrounded by ice. You'll even see mountains that pop their tops—volcanoes.

A volcano erupts when superhot melted rock, called magma, rises from inside the earth. Sometimes the magma works its way up through weak spots inside a mountain. Finally, it bursts through. At the surface, magma is called lava. Rivers of lava can destroy entire towns. But at the same time, the lava can build up land. At sea, layers of lava have created land where none existed.

Some mountains rise from the land. Others rise from the ocean floor. An ocean-based mountain can be taller than a land-based peak. Consider Hawaii's Mauna Kea (MOHW-nuh KAY-uh). Measured from the seafloor, it is almost a mile taller than Mount Everest. Read on to learn about these and other unique peaks.

▲ *These snowy peaks in southern Chile form part of the world's longest mountain chain above sea level: the Andes. The chain stretches 4,500 miles along the west coast of South America, down to the continent's southern tip. At the continent's northern tip, the chain connects to mountain ranges that extend through Alaska. Several peaks in the Andes set records for height. One, Mount Aconcagua (ak-uhn-KAHG-wuh), is the highest in the Americas.*

◀ *High and mighty, Mount Everest challenges climbers on a 1984 expedition. They stand on a rock-covered area called a moraine, in Asia's Himalayas. At 29,028 feet tall, Everest seems to scrape the sky. It is the tallest mountain above sea level. Many local people call it Qomolangma, "goddess mother of the world."*

GEO-QUIZ!

Can you name the highest mountain on each continent?

From highest to lowest, the mountains are: Mount Everest, in Asia; Mount Aconcagua, in South America; Mount McKinley, in North America; Kilimanjaro (kill-uh-muhn-JAHR-oh), in Africa; El'brus (el-BREWZ), in Europe; the Vinson Massif (VIN-suhn ma-SEEF), in Antarctica; and Mount Kosciusko (kahz-ee-UHS-koh), in Australia.

LAURIE HAMILTON

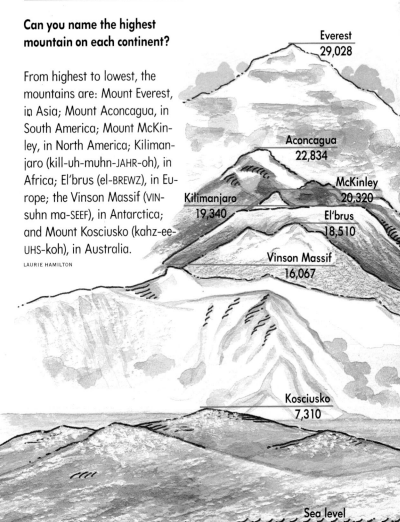

Everest
29,028

Aconcagua
22,834

McKinley
20,320

Kilimanjaro
19,340

El'brus
18,510

Vinson Massif
16,067

Kosciusko
7,310

Sea level
0

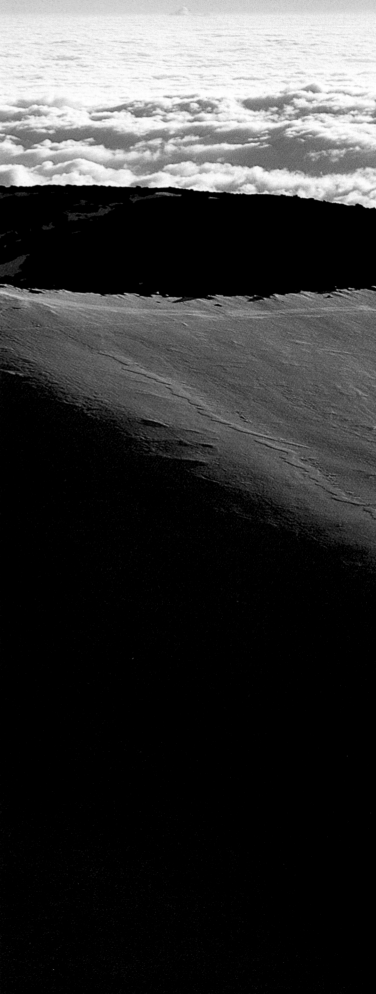

▲ *You don't have to be a mountain climber to explore some parts of the Alps — Europe's major mountain system. Ride in a cable car like one of these and climb in comfort. You'll start on a peak in France. On the way, you'll glimpse Mont Blanc (MAHNT BLAHNK), on the French-Italian border. It's the tallest mountain in the Alps and in western Europe. The ride ends on a peak in Italy.*

▶ *Whoosh! Skiers zoom down Mauna Kea, on the island of Hawaii. At the same time, the shores of the island are so warm that swimmers splash in the Pacific Ocean. Mauna Kea, once an active volcano, reaches 13,796 feet into the sky. That's not even the midpoint of Mount Everest. But there's more to Mauna Kea than meets the eye. Its base rests on the ocean floor. From base to top, it is 33,476 feet tall. That height outranks even Everest's.*

GEO-QUIZ!

In Greenland and Antarctica, thick sheets of ice cover huge mountains. Some peaks poke through the ice. Each of these bare peaks is called a polar ice cap. True or False?

False. Each bare peak is called a nunatak (NUHN-uh-tack). That's a Greenlandic Eskimo word for mountaintop surrounded by an ice sheet.

LAURIE HAMILTON

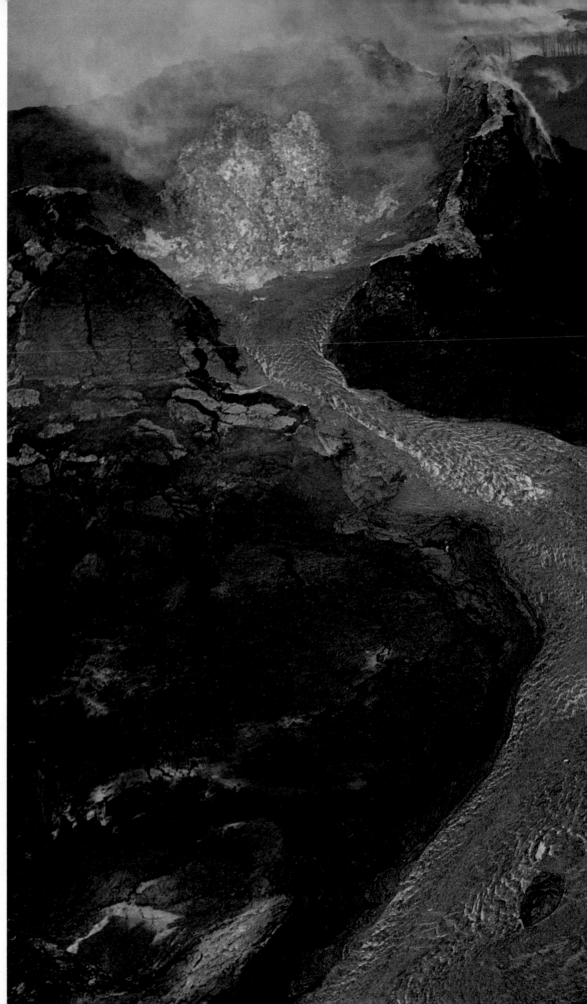

GEO-QUIZ!

The loudest sound ever recorded came from: A) a jet plane breaking the sound barrier, B) thunder in a tropical storm, or C) a volcanic eruption.

The correct choice is **C.** In 1883, a volcanic island called Krakatau erupted. The blast tore up much of the Indonesian island, which lies in a strait off the Indian Ocean. The explosion was so loud that people on an island nearly 3,000 miles away heard it. It sounded "like the distant roars of heavy guns," reported one islander.

LAURIE HAMILTON

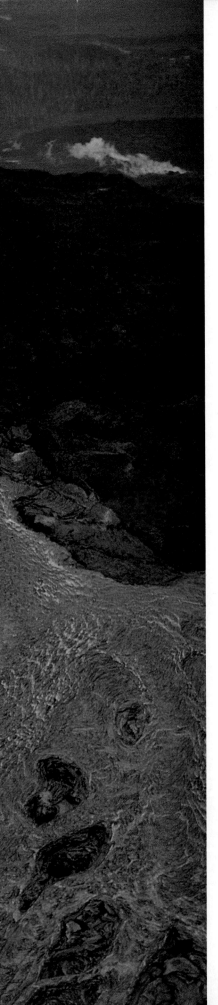

ROBERT S. PATTON, NATIONAL GEOGRAPHIC STAFF

◀ *Hawaii's Kilauea (key-lohw-AY-uh) volcano pours out glowing lava. Kilauea has erupted dozens of times in the past five years. That makes it one of the most active volcanoes in the world. Since 1983, enough lava has poured down its slopes to cover a four-lane highway stretching across the United States from coast to coast—to a depth of more than 30 feet. For centuries, many Hawaiians have said that Pele (pell-eh), goddess of volcanic fires, lives in Kilauea.*

K. AND M. KRAFFT

▲ *Two weeks old and growing, a volcanic mountain rises on the island of Heimaey (hay-MYE), part of Iceland. On January 23, 1973, fiery lava suddenly shot out of the earth near the island's only town. A volcano was born! For five months, the volcano continued to rumble and explode. By the time it quieted down on June 26, it had tossed out enough lava and ash to build a volcanic mountain 705 feet high. Lava extended the island's coastline by nearly one square mile. Scientists on Iceland named the volcano Eldfell, or "fire mountain."*

GEO-QUIZ!

The Ring of Fire is: A) a loop of volcanoes, B) a hot spot under the Himalayas, or C) a world-famous jewel.

The correct choice is **A**. Most of the world's active volcanoes form a loop around the Pacific Ocean. People call this loop the Ring of Fire. You'll find the volcanoes along the edges of plates. If you could count every volcano in the loop, your total would top 300. The picture below represents groups of volcanoes that help make up the Ring of Fire. In the Ring of Fire, volcanoes erupt frequently — sometimes at the same time. The forces that produce volcanic eruptions in the Ring of Fire also cause earthquakes there.

ASIA

NORTH AMERICA

SOUTH AMERICA

AUSTRALIA

PACIFIC OCEAN

◀ Steam rises from the crater atop Mount St. Helens, a part of the Ring of Fire. The volcano lies in the Cascade Range, in the northwestern United States. When Mount St. Helens blew its top in 1980, the eruption destroyed hundreds of square miles of surrounding forests. Ice and snow on the mountain melted instantly. Water gushed down the slopes, taking five and a half billion tons of mud, rocks, trees, and volcanic ash with it. Some of the mixture coated a valley below, raising its floor as much as 600 feet. Winds blew some ash around the world.

◀ With a thunderous blast, Mount Colo spits superhot lava, ash, and gases into the air. After a long sleep, the volcano erupted in 1983. Scientists predicted this eruption on the island of Unauna, in Indonesia. As a result, islanders were evacuated in time. Mount Colo is one of about 70 fiery mountains in Indonesia. This nation, made up of many islands, lies in southeast Asia. About one-seventh of the world's active volcanoes dot the islands.

Low, and Behold

ou've just climbed some of the world's highest mountains and some of the most fiery. Now catch your breath and tighten the laces on your climbing boots. You're about to hike another kind of land feature: a depression. Only this time, you'll be climbing *down* instead of up. Depressions are low areas of the earth's surface. You'll start at the Grand Canyon (right), in the southwestern United States. To explore it, you'll take a steep, four-hour hike to the bottom. Then you'll follow the winding Colorado River. It runs for 277 miles between the canyon walls.

What carved the Grand Canyon? Scientists give this explanation: Millions of years ago, forces in the earth pushed up the land that contains the canyon today. The area is now called the Colorado Plateau. Across the land ran the Colorado River. As the land slowly rose into a plateau, the river cut down through it. The combined action of rising and cutting created a deep canyon. As the river cut, it exposed layer after layer of rock.

Each layer of rock gives a clue to the earth's history. In layers near the top of the canyon, you'll see fossils of prehistoric sea creatures. In lower layers, you'll find some of the oldest rock on earth—almost two billion years old.

You could spend years exploring the Grand Canyon and other canyons on earth, but you've got another kind of depression to see—a rift valley. Water plays no part here. Land movement alone creates rift valleys. Here's how: Forces in the earth split the land, forming two parallel cracks. Between the cracks is a strip of land. Slowly, the cracks separate and the strip sinks, forming a valley floor. Land on either side of the strip forms valley walls.

The Great Rift Valley, in Asia and Africa, is a series of rift valleys. It is the longest rift valley system on land. The valley holds two other world records: the hottest place and the lowest place you can reach on land. After visiting these low-level areas, you'll have to climb up again to continue your journey. Ahead you'll discover that geography has many more ups and downs.

PATRICK MORROW

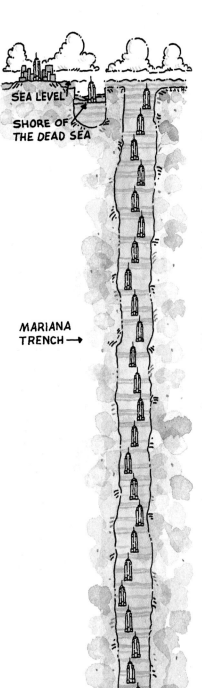

SEA LEVEL

SHORE OF
THE DEAD SEA

MARIANA
TRENCH →

MICHAEL COLLIER

▲ *Rafters on the Colorado River bounce over shallow Lava Falls, in the Grand Canyon. At the falls, the river rushes over a barrier of lava. About a million years ago, a volcano erupted near Toroweap Overlook. Lava flowed into the river and formed the barrier.*

◄ *A visitor at Toroweap Overlook, part of the Grand Canyon, gazes at the Colorado River 3,000 feet below. The fast-moving Colorado has helped shape the canyon over the past six to ten million years. Hard rains wash sand and gravel from the surrounding desert and from the canyon walls down into the river. The grains scrape and carve the canyon. This action deepens the canyon by a few inches every thousand years.*

GEO-QUIZ!

How low can you go on land? How deep can you sink to the bottom of the ocean?

The Dead Sea lies near the northern end of the Great Rift Valley, which runs through Asia and Africa. At 1,312 feet below sea level, the shore of the sea is the lowest spot you can reach on land—but not on earth. That honor belongs to the Mariana Trench, which plunges 35,810 feet beneath the surface of the Pacific Ocean. If the Empire State Building sat on the shore of the Dead Sea, only its television tower would poke above sea level. From the bottom of the Mariana Trench to sea level, you could stack up more than 24 Empire State Buildings!

LAURIE HAMILTON

▲ Salt and heat: These ingredients make up Africa's Danakil Depression—the hottest place on earth. Temperatures of 120°F and higher scorch the land. The depression, in the Great Rift Valley, dips nearly 400 feet below sea level. Studies show that the Red Sea once filled the area. Over time, the sea dried up in this region, leaving a thick layer of salt. The salt miners shown here built their dwelling from blocks of salt.

VICTOR ENGLEBERT

▲ Even with superstrong binoculars, you'd never see from one end of the Great Rift Valley to the other. A series of rift valleys, it stretches about 5,000 miles, from southwest Asia to southeast Africa. Each of its valleys formed when the surface of the earth split, creating two parallel cracks. Slowly, the cracks separated. A strip of land between the cracks sank, forming the valley floor. Land on either side of the strip formed the valley walls. The walls pull apart by a fraction of an inch each year. As this happens, the floor continues to sink. In one part of the valley, it is so low that ocean water seeps in. Scientists predict that eventually the floor will sink low enough for the ocean to flood the valley, dividing Africa in two.

At California's Death Valley National Monument, visitors gaze out on a land of opposites. At 282 feet below sea level, Death Valley is the lowest spot in the Americas. At 11,049 feet above sea level, Telescope Peak, in the background, pierces the sky. Death Valley is the driest spot in the United States. But here, rare rain has flooded it.

▼ When is a rock a scooter? When it scoots across Racetrack, a dry lake bed at Death Valley National Monument. Look at the skid marks. Some scientists think that many rocks tumble from nearby mountains. Then rain makes the ground slick, and gusty winds push the rocks.

Hidden Hollows

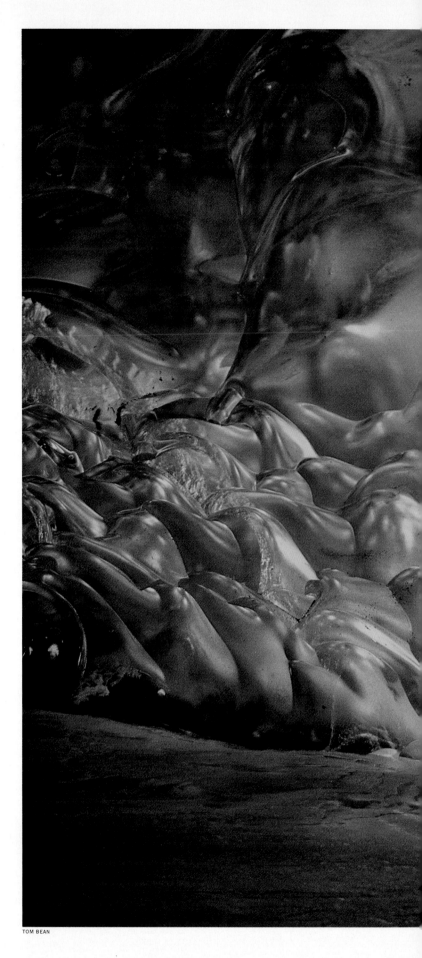

n the popular book *The Adventures of Tom Sawyer,* Tom, the main character, and his friend Becky lose their way in a dark cave. If they had been in an ice cave like this one, in Alaska, they would have had no trouble. Sunlight passes through the walls of an ice cave.

Unlike an underground cave, which forms in the earth, an ice cave usually forms inside an ice mass called a glacier. As glacial ice melts, it releases streams of water. These streams, combined with warm air, hollow out caves. Sometimes melted snow flowing from nearby mountains carves a cave in glacial ice. In summer, water and air may create a cave as wide as a three-car garage.

Water and air can carve underground caves, too. But the process is very different. Rainwater combines with carbon dioxide from the air and soil. This forms a weak acid solution. As the solution trickles into the earth, it eats away at limestone. Gradually, the solution hollows out a tunnel. New Zealand's Waitomo (wye-TOE-moe) Caves (opposite page) formed this way. How long does such cave-building take? Hundreds of thousands of years.

A lava tube cave takes shape in less time. It starts to form when lava streams out of a volcano and flows along the ground. In hours, the surface of the lava cools. Hot lava drains out, leaving a hollow tube of hardened lava. Eventually sections of the tube ceiling may collapse, forming chambers, or caves. Now you'll tour several caves, including parts of the world's longest cave system.

▶ *A hiker gazes at the pillow-shaped walls of an ice cave in Alaska. Streams of melted snow from nearby mountains helped hollow out this cave inside a huge chunk of ice. The chunk was part of Muir Glacier. Warm air melts and shapes the walls, changing them from week to week.*

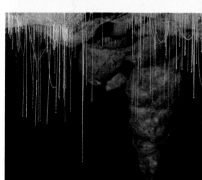

▲ *If you take a tour through Waitomo Caves, in New Zealand, hundreds of glowworms will help light the way (top). Waitomo means "water entering the cave." The caves formed as acidic rainwater seeped underground and slowly dissolved limestone. Today a stream runs through a part of the cave, called "Glowworm Grotto." There, glowworms cling to the walls and ceiling. To eat, they spin long, sticky threads (bottom) that trap flying insects, then reel them in.*

▲ It's a "lava-ly" picture. At Lava Beds National Monument, in California, a photographer sets off a series of camera flashes to light up a lava tube cave so he can photograph it. Compared with limestone caves, this cave and other lava tube caves near it took shape quickly. Centuries ago, hot lava spurted out of volcanoes and streamed over the land. The top layer of each stream cooled and hardened. The lava underneath remained hot and continued flowing, eventually draining away. Within weeks, only lava tubes were left. Over time, parts of their ceilings collapsed, forming caves. You'll find about 200 lava tube caves at Lava Beds National Monument.

▶ If these tourists at Kentucky's Mammoth Cave expect to see all of it in one visit, they'll have to make it a very long visit. Mammoth Cave—the longest known cave system on earth—stretches about 300 miles. To explore it would take weeks. Explorers wouldn't be bored. They'd see dozens of natural sculptures, such as these gigantic columns, called the Ruins of Karnak. They resemble ancient ruins at Karnak, in Egypt. The cave columns were sculpted by water. Once acidic rainwater has eaten through limestone and hollowed out a cave, more of the water runs down the cave walls, carving shapes in them. In other places, the water drips slowly, depositing minerals dissolved from the limestone. Some deposits, called stalactites, hang like icicles from the ceiling. Others, stalagmites, rise from the floor. These form as, year after year, the water drips from the ceiling, leaving minerals. On the floor, the minerals build up into stone columns.

CHIP CLARK

▲ On a tour through Mammoth Cave, you may see creatures that swim and crawl, but most of them won't see you. The blindfish (top) and the cave crayfish (bottom) are examples. In the darkness of the cave, they have no need for sight. Instead, they have highly developed senses of sound and touch that help them travel through the cave and find food. About 30 kinds of animals spend their entire lives in the cave. These include cave crickets and beetles.

CHIP CLARK

Ruins

Stories in Stone

Did you know that rocks can make interesting reading? By studying rocks in their surroundings, you can "read" stories about the earth. Scientists who read rocks have learned that mountains stand in places where the land was once flat, and that some deserts cover areas that were underwater. They've learned when dinosaurs roamed the earth.

What kinds of rocks do scientists read? Sometimes they read huge, single rocks, such as Uluru (OO-loo-roo)—also called Ayers Rock—in Australia (right). Sometimes they read groups of rocks, such as the rock towers in Bryce Canyon National Park (far right, top), in Utah. In every case, they seek clues that will tell them about the history of the rocks and of the earth nearby.

For example, Uluru's sandstone is more resistant than the rock surrounding it. Geologists found that the rock remained standing while wind and rain eroded the sandstone around it. The rocks at Bryce reveal that they started forming when layers of gravel, sand, and mud with lime piled up in and near ancient lakes. Slowly, the lakes dried up and the layers hardened into rock. As the area was later uplifted, the rocks cracked. Then rain, ice, and snow carved the exposed rock layers into towers.

Geologists find volumes of reading in the southwestern United States. There, miles of jagged rock walls form one of the most extensive canyon countries on earth. To read these rocky stories, read on.

▶ *Is it a hill? A mountain? It's Uluru—the world's biggest monolith, or single rock. Uluru, in Australia, stands more than 1,000 feet tall. Scientists think it was once part of a sandstone plateau. Wind and rain eroded the plateau, leaving Uluru and smaller monoliths nearby.*

▲ Can you top these? They're just a few of the thousands of rock towers and walls that touch the sky in Bryce Canyon National Park, in Utah. Iron and other metals combine with oxygen to color the rock. The structures are carved by rain, snow, and ice. As water freezes and expands in cracks in the rock, the rock crumbles. Rain and melting snow wash away bits of rock. This weakens the structures.

▲ Here's a challenge for you: Once you've climbed to the top of Uluru and down, take a hike around its base. That's an extra six miles. On the hike, you'll see caves in the rock. Paintings cover some cave walls. Aborigines, native Australians, painted the walls to tell their story of creation, called "Dreamtime."

◀ If you wanted to build a campfire, you'd steer clear of these logs. They're made of stone. Ancient rivers once ran through eastern Arizona. As they flooded, they picked up fallen trees and washed them into the area now called Petrified Forest National Park. Volcanic ash, mud, and sand buried the trees. Minerals in groundwater seeped into the wood, replacing it cell by cell. Much later, erosion uncovered the trees—and the world's largest petrified forest.

▲ According to an Indian legend, Devils Tower, in Wyoming, was once a low rock. One day a bear chased people onto the rock and it rose, lifting them to safety. The rock is 865 feet tall. It formed when magma filled the core of a volcano and hardened into a plug of rock. Wind and rain eroded the volcano. The plug remained.

▶ Ages ago, these sandstone cliffs on the Colorado Plateau were shifting sand dunes. Over time, a thick cover of lime, mud, and more sand buried them. Then chemicals in groundwater cemented their sand grains into rock. Much later, erosion exposed the rock and shaped it into cliffs.

26

▲ A worker chips away at a cliff to expose the bones of a dinosaur. Here at Dinosaur National Monument, on the border of Utah and Colorado, scientists have found the bones of prehistoric crocodiles, turtles, and many dinosaurs. The bones won't break easily. Over millions of years, minerals seeped into the bones, replacing their cells. Like the petrified logs, they are stone.

▼ Even a mountain goat couldn't keep up with this expert climber! She scales a 300-foot cliff a few miles from Canyonlands National Park, in Utah. Inside the park's 527-square-mile area, you'll find many of the canyons of the United States.

Shifting Sands

People who make their homes in the Western Desert (right), part of Africa's Sahara, worry about hot sun and shortages of water. They worry about dunes, too. These hills of sand are built by the wind. They take shape more quickly than other land features do. As dunes are being formed by the wind they may move across the land, covering objects in their path—even entire villages, such as this one.

You can find dunes where there is enough wind and enough sand. You'll find dunes at beaches and in hot deserts, such as the Sahara. You'll find them in cold, dry valleys, too, such as Victoria Valley, in Antarctica. Dunes in a frozen land? Yes! In Victoria Valley, there is enough sand so that dunes grow to about 30 feet tall. To find sand dunes made from a powdery, white mineral called gypsum (JIP-suhm), you can visit a gypsum dune field in New Mexico. To see some of the world's biggest dunes—almost as tall as the Washington Monument—you can walk along certain beaches in Oregon, or travel through China's Taklimakan (tahk-luh-muh-KAHN) Desert.

How does a dune form? It starts as wind blows sand grains over a surface. When the grains meet an obstacle such as a rock or a bump in the ground, they stop moving and begin to pile up. A dune may rise 30 feet or 300 feet. As the dune is forming, it may start to move. The wind keeps blowing, pushing grains up one side of the dune and down the other. The dune moves in the direction the wind is blowing.

Strong winds can move a dune almost a foot a day. That's an important figure for desert dwellers. The houses you see here will be slowly covered with sand. Residents will have to move to other towns.

Is there any way to stop the forward march of dunes? People have been trying for centuries. Along beaches, people plant grass to hold dunes in place. In deserts, they shove straw into the dunes to keep them from shifting. But these methods don't always work. Scientists are trying to come up with solutions. Can you think of some?

GEORG GERSTER

28

THOMAS J. ABERCROMBIE, NATIONAL GEOGRAPHIC STAFF

▲ Curved like a wave, a giant sand dune rises from the floor of Africa's Sahara, the largest hot desert on earth. The dune's height: 150 feet. A dune forms as wind blows sand across a surface. When the sand meets an obstacle, it stops. Gradually, it piles up.

◀ In the Western Desert of Egypt, moving sand dunes turn a busy oasis (oh-AY-sis) town into a ghost town. In places in the desert, rainwater collects underground and creates an oasis—a spot where the land can be farmed. Sometimes a village grows up at an oasis. When wind blows dunes across the oasis, villagers must leave. Slowly their homes will be covered with sand. In the Western Desert, some dunes move more than 300 feet a year. Today, satellite images show moving dunes. The images also reveal areas between the dunes that are safe for settlement.

▶ This is no snowy ride. At White Sands National Monument, in New Mexico, children zoom down a sand dune made of a mineral called gypsum. White Sands, a dune field, has the world's largest gypsum dunes. Some are as tall as a six-story building. Streams carry gypsum down from nearby mountains. As the water evaporates, the gypsum forms crystals. Eventually the crystals break down into grains. Wind blows the grains into dunes. Gypsum sand is lighter and softer than most sand, which is made of quartz. So a gypsum dune makes a good slide. To zip downhill, most sliders sit on waxed wooden boards.

NATIONAL GEOGRAPHIC PHOTOGRAPHER GEORGE F. MOBLEY

29

GEO-QUIZ!

Where can you hear the drum-beat of the dunes?

In some deserts, sand dunes make mysterious music. More than 700 years ago, when the 13th-century explorer Marco Polo traveled through western China's Taklimakan Desert, he heard the music. He wrote that it sounded much like drums. Studies show that sand grains in a musical dune are especially smooth. As a patch of sand slides down the dune, the motion produces low booming sounds similar to those made by drums and bass fiddles.

LAURIE HAMILTON

◀ *Did you spot the horseback riders? This towering sand dune makes them appear pint-size. Here, in the Chinese Pamirs (puh-MEERZ), mountains at the edge of the Taklimakan Desert, wind whips the sand into dunes hundreds of feet tall. The top of this dune is shaped like a pyramid. Winds in the Taklimakan and other deserts sometimes shape dunes into the forms of crescents, stars, straight lines, and curved swords. Many travelers have become lost among the huge dunes in this desert. For that reason, it was named Taklimakan, or "land of no return." One explorer, Marco Polo, did return. He brought news of giant dunes like this one to the western world.*

Land at Sea

Set sail! It's time to visit islands. For centuries, islands have been places of fantasy and adventure. Artists journeyed to Tahiti (right), in the South Pacific, to paint its colorful scenery and its people. Captain Kidd, a notorious pirate, once hid along the beaches of Madagascar, an island near the southeast coast of Africa. Maybe you recently traveled to an island for a family vacation.

All islands are small areas of land surrounded by water. You can find them in oceans, in lakes, or in rivers. They can be very different from one another. Tahiti is a volcanic island. It formed when lava built up two volcanoes from the ocean floor. At the water's surface, the two lava flows joined and hardened into an island. Below you see Rose Atoll (AT-tawl), another kind of island in the South Pacific. An atoll forms when tiny sea creatures called corals attach to the sides of an ocean-based volcano. When they die, their limestone skeletons remain. More corals attach to these. Over thousands of years, the skeletons stack up, and a coral ring builds to the water's surface. Slowly, the ocean floor sinks into the earth's crust, pulling the volcano's peak underwater. The corals continue to build, so that a ring always juts above the water's surface.

As you sail around the world, you'll see ice-covered islands, such as Greenland, in the North Atlantic Ocean. You'll see islands with forests of pine, such as Madeline Island, in North America's Lake Superior. You'll see hundreds of others, too. On each one, adventure awaits.

◄ *This South Pacific island, called Rose Atoll, is made partly of tiny sea creatures. An atoll forms when corals attach to the sides of a volcano. As the corals die, their skeletons build up a ring at the water's surface. If the volcano sinks, a ring remains, as at Rose Atoll.*

GEO-QUIZ!

What island nation consists of more than 10,000 islands?

The nation of Indonesia has 13,667 islands within its boundaries. Many of the islands are only about one square mile in area. You could cross each in no time. Going from one end of the nation to the other would be a different story. The islands spread for more than 3,000 miles across the Pacific.

LAURIE HAMILTON

◀ *Meet Tahiti. Many people have called this island "Queen of the Pacific." Why? For centuries, its scenery has charmed writers, painters, and explorers. Tahiti formed when lava built up two volcanoes from the ocean floor. At the water's surface, the lava flows joined. Over time, vegetation grew, perhaps from seeds carried by birds or by the wind.*

NICHOLAS DEVORE III/PHOTOGRAPHERS ASPEN

33

Go with the flow! A surfer rides a wave off the Hawaiian island of Oahu. Wind and water conditions here create the kind of wave that surfers often seek. Some people call Honolulu, Oahu's major city, the birthplace of modern surfing.

'Waterful' Worlds

INTRODUCTION

2 Surf's up! Off the coast of Oahu, in Hawaii, a surfer races along on a moving wall of water. Hawaii is a surfer's paradise. It's surrounded by water. You'll find many giant waves. Still, some surfers search throughout the world for "the perfect wave." There are a lot of places to look. Turn the page and study the map. The entire blue area is water, and much of that water has good waves for surfing.

Almost three-quarters of the earth's surface is made up of water. Oceans hold most of it. Water evaporates from the ocean, falls to earth as rain or snow, flows back to the ocean through rivers and streams, and evaporates again. The cycle never ends.

You can surf on the ocean, and you can sail on the ocean, but you cannot drink water directly from it. It's too salty. Less than three percent of the world's water is fresh. Most of that is frozen solid, locked into glaciers and ice caps. The fresh water that people can use makes up less than one percent of all the water on earth.

On the following pages, you'll explore waters from Iceland to Africa. As you discover deep oceans, long rivers, and towering icebergs, you'll find that one thing is true: Water is on the move. A wave crashes against a coastline. A geyser skyrockets into the air. A waterfall tumbles hundreds of feet and thunders against a basin of rocks. A glacier rumbles and cracks. In oceans, currents carry water from the tropics to the polar regions, and back again.

As you explore, keep this in mind: There's more to water than motion. To really find out about the bodies of water on earth, you'll have to hold your breath and dive into them. Below the surface of almost every lake, river, and ocean, you'll find a world complete with plants and animals—many you've never seen before. Believe it or not, you share a common bond with every one of these creatures. What is it? Like the earth itself, every living thing on it is made mostly of water. That includes you!

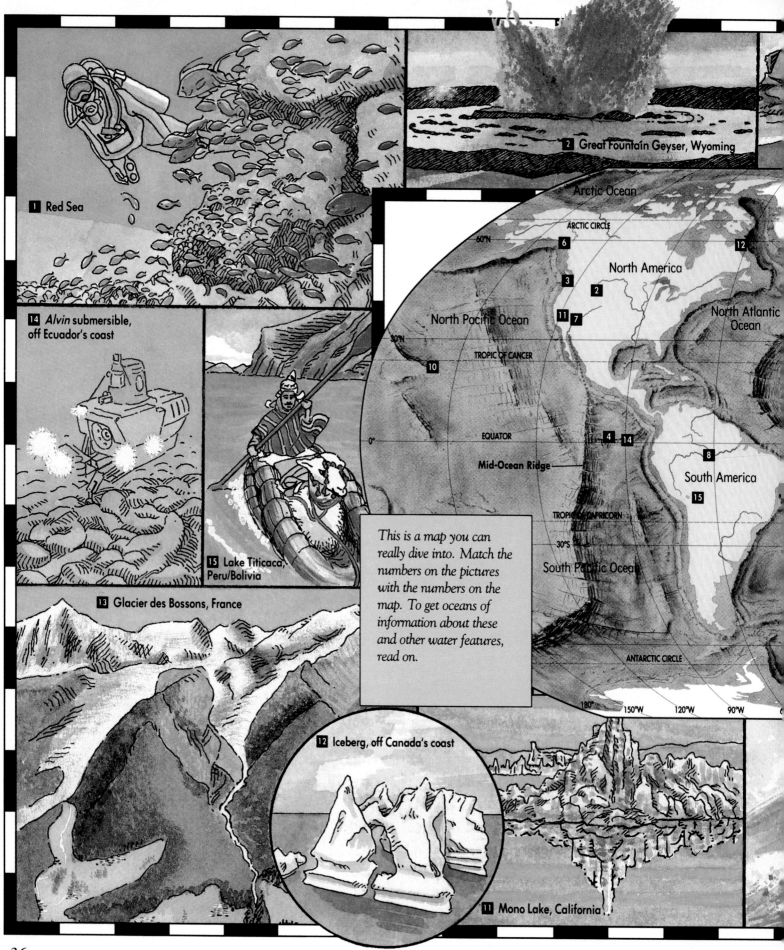

1 Red Sea

2 Great Fountain Geyser, Wyoming

14 *Alvin* submersible, off Ecuador's coast

15 Lake Titicaca, Peru/Bolivia

13 Glacier des Bossons, France

This is a map you can really dive into. Match the numbers on the pictures with the numbers on the map. To get oceans of information about these and other water features, read on.

Arctic Ocean

ARCTIC CIRCLE

60°N   6

North America

3

2

North Pacific Ocean

North Atlantic Ocean

11 7

30°N

TROPIC OF CANCER

10

EQUATOR

Mid-Ocean Ridge

4 14

South America

8

15

TROPIC OF CAPRICORN

30°S

South Pacific Ocean

ANTARCTIC CIRCLE

180°   150°W   120°W   90°W

12 Iceberg, off Canada's coast

11 Mono Lake, California

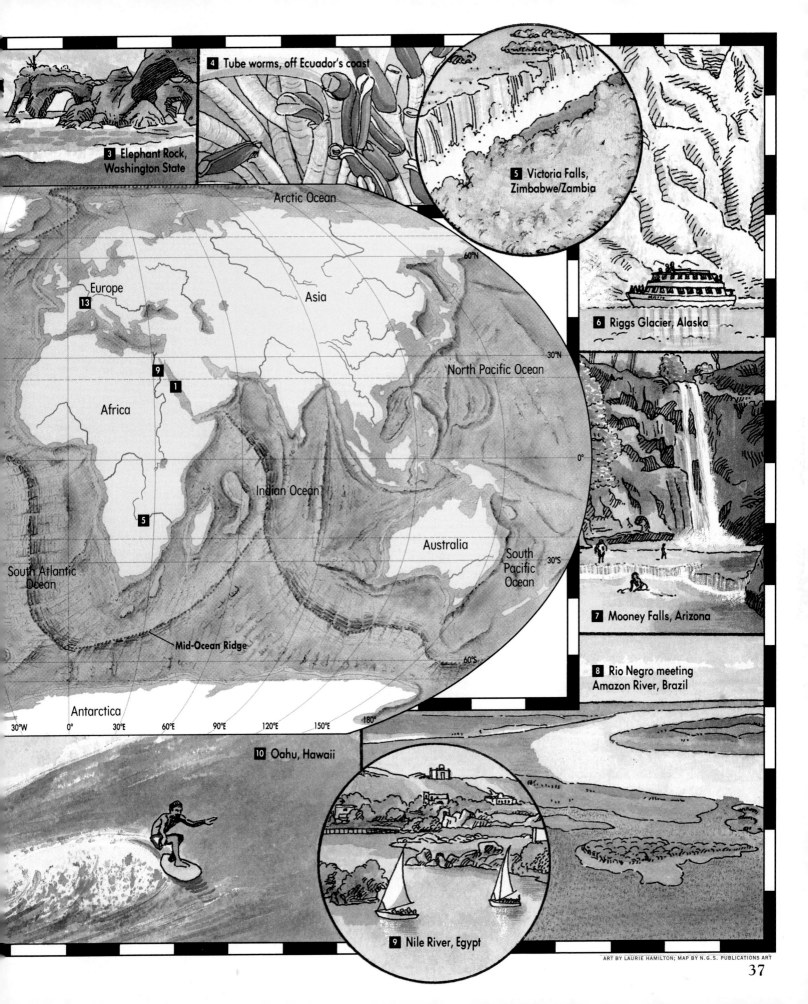

4 Tube worms, off Ecuador's coast

3 Elephant Rock, Washington State

5 Victoria Falls, Zimbabwe/Zambia

6 Riggs Glacier, Alaska

Arctic Ocean

60°N

Europe

13

Asia

30°N

North Pacific Ocean

9

1

Africa

0°

Indian Ocean

5

Australia

South Pacific Ocean

30°S

South Atlantic Ocean

Mid-Ocean Ridge

60°S

7 Mooney Falls, Arizona

8 Rio Negro meeting Amazon River, Brazil

Antarctica

30°W   0°   30°E   60°E   90°E   120°E   150°E   180°

10 Oahu, Hawaii

9 Nile River, Egypt

ART BY LAURIE HAMILTON; MAP BY N.G.S. PUBLICATIONS ART

By the Sea, In the Sea

J ules Verne, an author who lived in the 1800s, wrote a fantasy about exploring the ocean depths. Its title: *Twenty Thousand Leagues Under the Sea*. In the story, a sea captain and his crew journey about 50,000 miles through the ocean in a submarine and discover amazing sea creatures.

Verne wrote his story from imagination. Little did he know how close it was to future reality. Since the 1950s, scientists have been living similar adventures. Some explore the ocean alone. Wearing scuba gear, they swim as deep as 300 feet. Others climb into underwater vehicles called submersibles to explore at deeper levels. One submersible descended almost seven miles below the ocean's surface. None of the scientists travel as far as Verne's characters did. But the modern expeditions are every bit as exciting. The scientists observe and photograph unusual underwater plants and animals. They watch seaweed grow as much as two feet a day. They take close looks at giant tube worms attached to the ocean floor. They film sailfish that zip through the water at 65 miles an hour. They study a fish that changes from female to male. They record the behavior of gigantic blue whales, each weighing more than 25 elephants.

The explorers see unusual landscapes, too—deep valleys and high mountains. These features have been formed by forces inside the earth, just as mountains and valleys on dry land have been formed. Some of these features are more surprising than the land features. Did you know, for instance, that the world's longest mountain range is under the ocean?

In this book, you'll notice that some large bodies of water are called seas and others are called oceans. Seas, such as the Mediterranean Sea, between Europe and Africa, or the Red Sea, between Africa and Asia, are small versions of oceans. Many resemble huge bays and are surrounded almost completely by land. Most seas connect to one of the four oceans: the Pacific, the Atlantic, the Indian, or the Arctic. Each ocean and sea holds a world of wonder for explorers. To start *your* fantastic voyage, plunge in!

▶ A scuba diver explores the Red Sea, an arm of the Indian Ocean. There he finds some of the most unusual plants and animals in the underwater world. These fish are just one example. The females have the ability to turn into males. Take a look at the colorful coral reefs, too. These form as corals attach themselves to the seafloor. Over time, the corals' skeletons stack up, forming reefs. Dozens of kinds of corals live in the Red Sea. Reddish algae grow there, too. At different times of the year, the plants collect at the surface, coloring the Red Sea...red.

PETER SCOONES/PLANET EARTH PICTURES

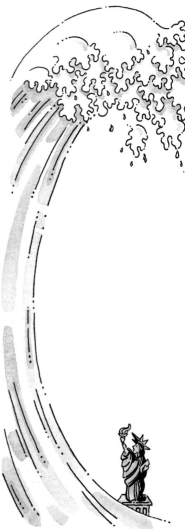

GEO-QUIZ!

The tallest wave on record was caused by a volcanic eruption. True or False?

False. In 1958, a landslide in southern Alaska plunged into a bay. The force created a wave 1,700 feet tall. That's five and a half times the height of the Statue of Liberty. Such a wave is called a tsunami (soo-NAH-mee). The word, from Japan, means "great harbor wave."

LAURIE HAMILTON

▲ *How about a hike on Heron Island? The island is part of Australia's Great Barrier Reef—the world's largest structure made of coral. On Heron Island, adventure begins when you step out of your hotel room onto the island's coral surface. At low tide, you can walk along connecting reefs. You'll explore long stretches of coral sculptures. When the tide is high, you can put on your snorkeling gear and view the coral underwater. As you swim, you'll see many unusual creatures. Hundreds of green turtles make their home off Heron's shore. You'll find sponges, sea cucumbers, and sea grapes, too.*

◀ A coral jungle spreads out before an observer on the Great Barrier Reef. If you joined her and explored the rest of the reef, you could count more than 400 kinds of corals, in many colors and shapes. The Great Barrier Reef extends 1,250 miles off the northeast coast of Australia. Along it, you can find the greatest variety of sea creatures on earth. About 1,500 kinds of fish swim in its waters. That's not all. If you searched carefully, you might spot a sea snake, an octopus—or a giant clam that weighs 500 pounds.

▶ You've probably heard of a sea horse. But have you ever heard of a sea elephant? Look closely at the rock in the middle of this picture. Do you see the shape of an elephant with its trunk in the water? Can you see other shapes in the rocks nearby? You'll find these stone sculptures on the Pacific coast, in Washington State. Over the years, waves eroded the rocks into works of art.

▶ You may have walked through a forest, but have you ever sailed through one? Here, in the Pacific Ocean off the coast of California, boats often cruise through a forest that grows underwater. Its "trees" are huge strands of seaweed called giant kelp. Kelp, which is attached to the seafloor, grows faster than any other marine plant. A strand of it may climb as much as two feet in one day. It may grow as tall as 200 feet. When the kelp shown here is full grown, workers aboard large ships will harvest it for commercial use. In 1986, about 100,000 tons of the kelp were collected.

▶ The next time you brush your teeth, think about kelp. Strands of kelp, such as these, produce a chemical called algin (AL-jin). Manufacturers put algin in toothpaste to make it smooth. Algin is also used to thicken products, such as dyes that color cloth. The whole kelp strand has its use, too. People who raise shellfish called abalone feed them kelp.

©FRED BAVENDAM/PETER ARNOLD, INC.

▲ Can you find two animals here? One is the shrimp, in the center. The other is the animal the shrimp is perched on—a sea anemone (uh-NEM-uh-nee). The anemone, a cousin of coral, has stinging tentacles that look somewhat like flower petals. If a small fish swims by, the anemone grabs it and shoves it into the mouth at the center of its tentacles. This kind of shrimp is safe. It lives on the anemone. Scientists think it eats dead tissue from the tentacles, helping the anemone to stay healthy. In return, the anemone leaves the shrimp alone and protects it from hungry fish.

▲ You don't have to be a scuba diver to explore underwater worlds. If you visit Grand Cayman Island, in the Caribbean Sea, you can observe life on a coral reef— and much more—through the portholes of Atlantis I. It's the first submarine built for tourists. For about an hour, you'll cruise 150 feet below the surface in the submarine's air-conditioned cabin. The water of the Caribbean is crystal clear, so you'll see many creatures, such as anemones and shrimp. You'll see sharks, turtles, and rainbow-colored tropical fish, too. Floodlights on the bottom of the sub show off the colors of the creatures. Atlantis I holds 28 people.

▲ *Worms, worms, worms, but not your ordinary kind! These have no eyes, no mouths—and they're 12 feet long. Scientists aboard Alvin spotted the creatures attached to the ocean floor in clumps. A closer look showed that the worms live near chimney-like vents. Hot water, rich in minerals, bubbles up from inside the earth and spurts through the vents. To eat, the worms absorb the minerals. Then bacteria inside the worms change the minerals into food.*

◀ *"Awesome!" That's how this boy aboard Atlantis I might describe his view of a Caribbean coral reef. Using one of the charts on the bench, he identifies some of the fish that swim along the reef. Another chart will help him recognize sponge gardens and coral formations. If he peers beyond the point where the coral reef drops off, he might see stingrays, sea turtles, sharks, and eels.*

▲ *What's it like to study the bottom of the ocean in this craft? One scientist said that it's like exploring the Grand Canyon at night with a flashlight. The craft, named Alvin, is called a submersible. It can dive more than two miles below the ocean's surface. At that dark depth, explorers have a hard time seeing the scenery, but special equipment helps them collect information. Underwater cameras take clear pictures of the ocean floor. Mechanical hands collect rocks and animals for later study. One find: a foot-long clam that grows 500 times faster than any other clam.*

GEO-QUIZ!

The longest mountain range on earth is A) the Andes, B) the Mid-Ocean Ridge, or C) the Himalayas.

The correct choice is **B.** The Mid-Ocean Ridge stretches for 46,000 miles along the bottom of the world's oceans. It winds around the globe like the seam on a baseball. The Himalayas, Andes, Alps, and Rockies placed end to end would be shorter than the ridge.

Flow Motion

**D**on't dry off yet! You've just explored most of the water on earth—in the oceans. Now it's time to explore rivers and lakes. Compared with oceans, these bodies of water may seem pint-size, but in their own way, they're just as important. People everywhere depend on them.

Some of the busiest cities in the world—including Paris, New York, Chicago, and London—have grown up near rivers and lakes. Why? Rivers and lakes provide fish for food and water for drinking. They provide pathways for ships to carry goods. The list goes on and on.

How does a lake get its start? In many cases, rain and snow collect in a basin carved by a moving glacier. Many rivers start on a mountain or other high place. As rain falls and snow melts, excess water builds up on the land. This water creates a stream that eventually flows into another stream. More streams feed into this one, and its flow increases. Gradually, the stream develops into a river.

Turn the page and visit Mono Lake, in California—a salt lake filled with goblin-like formations. Then float down South America's Amazon River. More than one thousand other rivers and streams flow into it.

GEO-QUIZ!

Sharks can live in lakes. True or False?

True. Even though all sharks swim in oceans, which contain salt water, one kind, the bull shark, also lives in freshwater lakes. Bull sharks swim up the San Juan River from the Caribbean Sea to reach Central America's Lake Nicaragua.

LAURIE HAMILTON

44

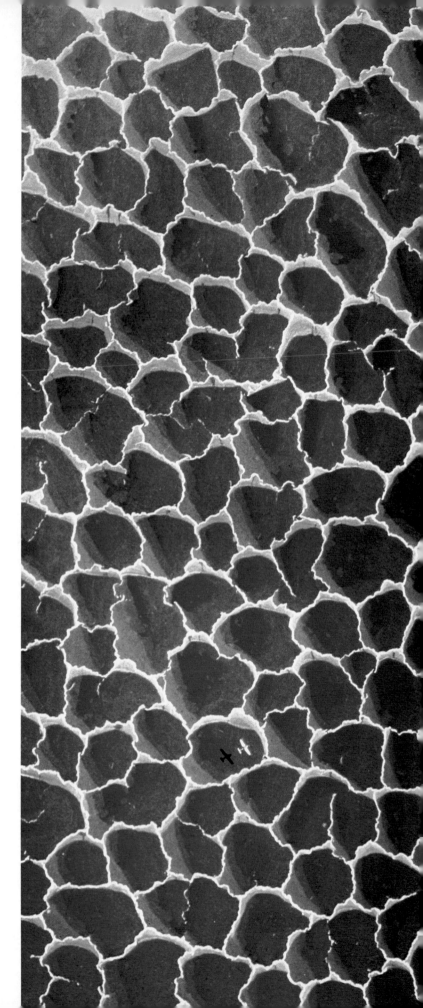

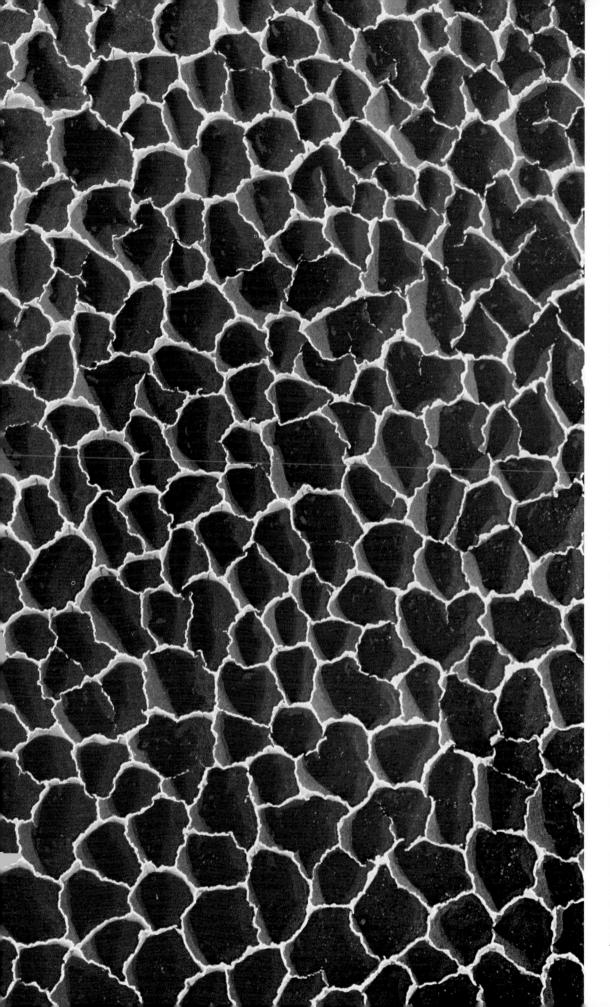

▲ Headed for a tribal ceremony that will use this llama, an Aymara (eye-muh-RAH) Indian paddles across Lake Titicaca (tih-tih-KAHK-uh), in South America. Lake Titicaca lies on the border between Bolivia and Peru, in the Andes. Nearly two and a half miles above sea level, it is the world's highest navigable lake. That means it is deep enough for large ships, such as passenger steamers, to cross.

◄ Passengers in the plane at lower left can see mineral deposits covering the floor of Tanzania's Lake Natron, in Africa. Natron is a soda lake. Hot springs on the lake floor spurt soda into it. Streams feed into it, dumping more soda, along with other minerals dissolved from rocks. Natron has no outlets. The minerals pour in—and stay. Gradually, they become concentrated, and pile up. Natron's color comes from bacteria that live there.

GEORG GERSTER

▲ Almost seven thousand years ago, Oregon's Crater Lake wasn't a lake at all. In its place stood a volcano that had erupted from time to time for about half a million years. Crater Lake got its start with the final major eruption. The blast was so violent that cinder and ash scattered over what are now eight states and three Canadian provinces. The volcanic peak caved in, leaving a basin about 6 miles wide and 2,000 feet deep. Over time, snow and rain filled it. Crater Lake—the deepest lake in the United States—was born.

▶ Goblins? Fairy castles? That's what some people have called these structures at Mono Lake, a salt lake in California. Scientists call them tufa (TYEW-fuh) towers. Tufa is mineral rock that is porous, or filled with holes. These towers formed as underwater springs spurted calcium onto Mono's floor. Gradually, the calcium combined with carbonate, another mineral in the lake. The minerals piled up and hardened. Los Angeles uses water from streams that flow into Mono. This has lowered the lake, exposing the rocks.

HARALD SUND/THE IMAGE BANK

▲ Sturdy sailboats called feluccas (fuh-LOO-kuhz) cruise the Nile River, in Egypt, in northeast Africa. The world's longest river, the Nile flows more than 4,000 miles through seven countries. Homes line the banks you see above. Along other parts of the river, you'll see temples and tombs. Much of the Nile runs through the Sahara. Irrigated farms line the banks, with desert stretching beyond.

▼ The dark, vegetation-stained waters of the Rio Negro (NEHG-row), in the foreground, join the muddy waters of the Amazon River. The meeting place: Brazil, in South America. A thousand rivers and streams flow into the Amazon. It carries more water than the world's seven other major rivers combined.

▼ A young girl stretches out on a giant lily pad in the Amazon River. If she's settling down for a nap, she's in for a surprise. The lily pad may look sturdy, but after a few minutes, it will sink under her weight. Then she can jump into the shallow water. If you followed the Amazon across Brazil, you'd see hundreds of giant lily pads—and more. The river passes through the world's largest tropical rain forest. It shelters hundreds of kinds of plants and animals.

Water: Its Ups And Downs

t roars. It foams. It plunges thousands of feet to earth and crashes against big boulders. It's Angel Falls (right). Just imagine Jimmy Angel's thrill when he spotted it tumbling down this mountainside in Venezuela, in South America.

The year: 1935. Angel, an adventurer, was looking for gold, not for water. But this discovery paid off. It made him famous. He had found the world's highest waterfall.

Water has some powerful ups and downs. A waterfall—water crashing down a mountain or a gorge—is one kind of power trip. A geyser—water blasting into the air—is another. At Yellowstone National Park, in Wyoming, Steamboat Geyser rockets water as high as a 40-story building. The water has lifted rocks and hurled them almost a hundred feet.

Where do such waterworks come from? A waterfall forms when a river or stream drops abruptly from a high level to a lower one. A waterfall may be 3 or 3,000 feet high. The higher ones can be the most spectacular—and the most dangerous. At Niagara Falls, on the border between the United States and Canada, the force of the rushing water erodes rocks below. Often boats must carry cargo along rivers with high waterfalls. How do they do it? They travel on canals that lead from the river, around the falls, and back to the river.

Geysers form after water seeps deep into the ground through narrow, twisting tunnels. Red-hot magma beneath the earth's surface heats the water. The hot water heats other water closer to the surface. This water boils and turns to steam. Pressure builds up until boiling water and steam burst out of the ground as a geyser. Some geysers may shoot up only a few feet. Others, inactive today, have surged as high as a thousand feet.

At Yellowstone, magma lies less than four miles underground. That's closer to the surface than in most other places. About half of the park's more than 200 geysers erupt in an area less than one mile square. Why not head in that direction and check them out? Just turn the page. On the way, you'll stop at Niagara for a look at the falls.

▲ Water rushes down the Niagara River and plunges over steep cliffs. Welcome to Niagara Falls! On the border between the United States and Canada, the falls tumble over rocks in two places. You can see American Falls, in New York, at top left, and Horseshoe Falls, in Ontario, at bottom left. About 20,000 bathtubsful of water pour over Niagara every second.

◀ Near the bottom of Niagara's American Falls, visitors get a closeup view of the pounding water. Yellow slickers keep them dry. About four million tourists visit the falls each year. Some climb to observation platforms like this one. Others take passenger steamers through the mist and foaming water at the base of the falls. There they see huge boulders that fell from the top ledge when the water's force eroded softer rock underneath.

▼ Splish, splash! Havasupai (hah-vah-SOO-pye) Indian children go for a dip in Havasu Creek, in the Grand Canyon. Behind them, Mooney Falls provides a gentle shower. Mooney is one of three falls on this Arizona creek, which runs through the isolated Havasupai reservation. Havasupai means "people of the blue-green water"—the color of the falls.

◀ A small plane takes sightseers close to the highest waterfall on earth, Angel Falls, in Venezuela, a country in South America. Angel Falls drops 3,212 feet over the side of Devil Mountain. In 1935, a gold seeker named Jimmy Angel sighted the falls. He named it after himself.

PAUL CHESLEY/PHOTOGRAPHERS ASPEN

▲ Clouds of mist drift upward from Victoria Falls, in southern Africa. In most cases, a waterfall pours down in a narrow stream. Victoria Falls spreads for a mile because the Zambezi River is a mile wide at the place where it spills over the side of a long gorge. In 1855, an explorer named the falls for Queen Victoria of England. Local people call it "smoke that thunders."

▲ A dome of water bubbles from Strokkur (STROH-kur) Geyser, in Iceland. In a few seconds, boiling water and steam will shoot out of the geyser as high as 82 feet. If visitors to Strokkur miss one eruption, they don't have to wait long for another. Strokkur spurts every 10 to 15 minutes. Fifteen geysers erupt within a ten-mile circle in Iceland. The term "geyser" comes from the Icelandic word geysir, which means "gusher."

▶ Moments ago, all was calm on the surface of this pool. Suddenly, great jets of water skyrocketed 150 feet into the air. What happened? Great Fountain Geyser erupted. You wouldn't care to drink from this giant water fountain. Its temperature is a scalding 200°F. Great Fountain is in Yellowstone National Park, in Wyoming. Some 200 geysers—more than anywhere else on earth—spurt and spray in Yellowstone.

GEO-QUIZ!

The world's highest-spouting geyser is called Old Faithful. True or False?

False. For more than 25 years, Steamboat Geyser, in Yellowstone National Park, has held the world record as the highest-spouting geyser. It sometimes shoots water 400 feet into the air. People never know when Steamboat will let off steam. But they have faith in Old Faithful. That Yellowstone geyser, which spurts water up to 130 feet, erupts every 33 to 120 minutes. It has stuck to schedule for more than 100 years.

LAURIE HAMILTON

Deep Freezes

When you think of fresh water, you might think of rushing rivers, or of the water that gushes from your tap. But three-quarters of the world's fresh water usually inches along at a pace slower than a snail's. It is frozen solid, locked into glaciers that cover about one-tenth of earth's land.

A glacier forms in a place where snow piles up faster than it melts. Over time, the snow turns into ice. When the ice is thick enough, its own weight causes it to move. Then it is called a glacier. A glacier may creep to an ocean or lake, sometimes forming a cliff at the water's edge. As the glacier moves forward, chunks break off and fall in. These chunks, called icebergs, may jut 500 feet above the water. That's about one-eighth of the berg. The rest may extend thousands of feet underwater. Sailors stay away from icebergs. As tough as steel, they can rip through a ship and quickly sink it. So as you explore waters near Iceberg Alley, on page 54, be on the lookout.

▼ *Like cake icing, Glacier des Bossons (day baw-SOWN) and other glaciers spread across peaks in the French Alps. As the glaciers melt in the warm air, water runs into the valley below, helping keep it green. Some 18,000 years ago, glaciers covered about one-third of the earth.*

▶ *Tourists on this cruise in Alaska's Glacier Bay National Park can hear Riggs Glacier rumble and roar as chunks of ice break off and drop into the water. The chunks are called icebergs. Alaska has about 100,000 glaciers. That makes the state one of the iciest places in the world.*

JEAN-PAUL FERRERO/AUSCAPE

TOM BEAN

GEO-QUIZ!

How big was the biggest iceberg ever accurately recorded?

In 1987, scientists spotted a monster berg floating in the Ross Sea, off the coast of Antarctica. It measured about 98 miles long and 25 miles wide. That's about twice the size of the state of Rhode Island. It had broken away from the Antarctic continent, which is covered almost completely by glacial ice. Icebergs from Antarctica are the largest in the world.

LAURIE HAMILTON

53

▲ They're off to see . . . the longest glacier in the Alps. The Aletsch (AH-letch) Glacier, in the Swiss Alps, is a whopping 15 miles long. Its average thickness is about 500 feet. Aletsch, called a valley glacier, creeps downhill at the rate of about 1½ feet every day. On its journey, it carries rock that ranges in size from tiny particles to giant boulders. Scientists have learned much about the movement of glaciers by studying them in the Alps.

▶ You'd need a big glass to hold this piece of ice. It's about as tall as a ten-story building. This iceberg floats off the coast of Canada, in a bay of the Labrador Sea. Here you see about one-eighth of it. Like other icebergs, most of it lies underwater. Near the bay is a stretch of water called Iceberg Alley. It has many bergs like this one. In 1912, the luxury liner Titanic hit an iceberg in the alley and sank. Two years later, patrollers began scanning the area to warn ships of bergs. The work continues today.

JOHN EASTCOTT AND YVA MOMATIUK/DRK PHOTO

GEO-QUIZ!

The only difference between the iciest regions on earth—the Arctic and the Antarctic—is that they lie at opposite ends of the earth. True or False?

False. These icy regions are different in many ways. Both are cold, but Antarctica is much colder. Both have periods of total sunlight or darkness, but at different times of the year. Ice covers much of both regions. The ice at the South Pole, in Antarctica, is glacial ice. It sits on land. But the ice over the North Pole, in the Arctic, is sea ice. It floats on the Arctic Ocean. Many animals thrive in the Arctic, including the polar bear. It is the biggest land animal there. But in Antarctica, the biggest land animal is a tiny, wingless insect, called *Belgica antarctica*. In a zoo, you might find polar bears and penguins living near each other. In the wild, however, you'll see polar bears only in the Arctic. No penguins live anywhere near these bears, but plenty of them live in Antarctica. The North Pole was the first to be reached by explorers—in 1909. In 1911, other explorers set foot on the South Pole.

THE ARCTIC

Arctic Tern

Polar Bear

1909

Arctic Hare

Walrus

Wolf

Ringed Seal

ANTARCTICA

Albatross

1911

Southern Elephant Seal

Leopard Seal

Belgica Antarctica

Adélie Penguins

Brrrr! Many parents wouldn't consider raising their babies out in the cold. But for emperor penguins, this icy plain in Antarctica makes a perfect nursery. Most adult penguins here are keeping chicks warm. Thousands of penguins may join a cool nursery.

Land Alive

Now that you've toured the earth's landforms and explored its waters, you're on your way to becoming a full-fledged geo-whiz. Your next step: to take a closeup look at life on earth. Many natural communities dot the surface of the earth. Each has certain plants and animals. Each has a climate that suits those plants and animals. Scientists call such communities biomes (BY-ohmz). To start finding out about biomes, just step outside. There, you might see robins or crows. Chances are, you wouldn't see penguins like those at left. You probably wouldn't see a landscape of ice, either. You might see trees and grass. That's because you live in one kind of biome, and penguins live in another.

Why is your biome different from a penguin's? It has a lot to do with the distance of your home—and the penguin's—from the Equator. Take a look at the map on the next pages. The lines that run across it horizontally are called lines of latitude. The center line is the Equator. At latitudes near the Equator, most temperatures are warm year-round. You find hot deserts and steamy rain forests. As you travel away from the Equator and toward the North or South Poles, average temperatures at each latitude grow cooler. At the Poles, temperatures remain extremely cold for most of the year. You probably live at a middle latitude between the Equator and the North Pole. These penguins live near the South Pole. In this chapter, you'll find out why temperatures differ at each latitude.

The latitude of a biome helps determine its climate, or average weather pattern over many years. In turn, a biome's climate influences the kinds of animals and plants that can live there. For example, penguins live comfortably in the icy climate near the South Pole. They have thick coats of feathers. But they'd roast in a hot desert.

In this book, you'll visit five major biomes. Each can be divided into several smaller biomes. Why not start your trip by locating the five biomes on the chapter map?

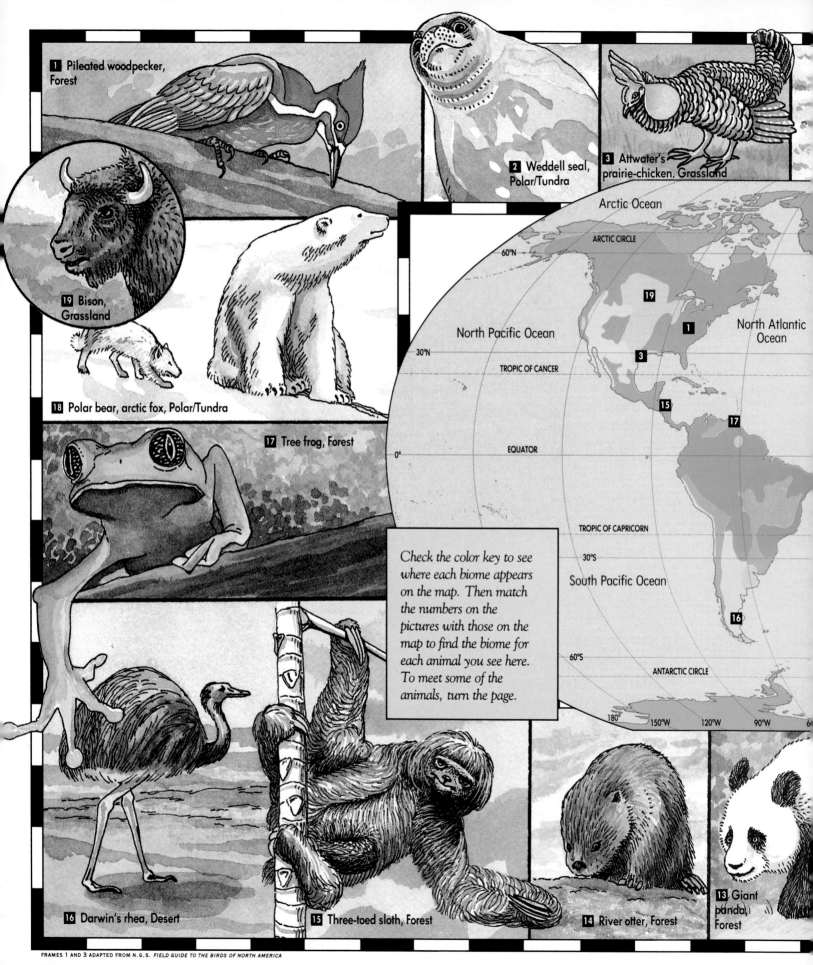

1 Pileated woodpecker, Forest

2 Weddell seal, Polar/Tundra

3 Attwater's prairie-chicken, Grassland

19 Bison, Grassland

18 Polar bear, arctic fox, Polar/Tundra

17 Tree frog, Forest

Check the color key to see where each biome appears on the map. Then match the numbers on the pictures with those on the map to find the biome for each animal you see here. To meet some of the animals, turn the page.

Arctic Ocean

ARCTIC CIRCLE

60°N

North Pacific Ocean

North Atlantic Ocean

30°N

TROPIC OF CANCER

EQUATOR

TROPIC OF CAPRICORN

30°S

South Pacific Ocean

60°S

ANTARCTIC CIRCLE

180°   150°W   120°W   90°W

16 Darwin's rhea, Desert

15 Three-toed sloth, Forest

14 River otter, Forest

13 Giant panda, Forest

FRAMES 1 AND 3 ADAPTED FROM N.G.S. *FIELD GUIDE TO THE BIRDS OF NORTH AMERICA*

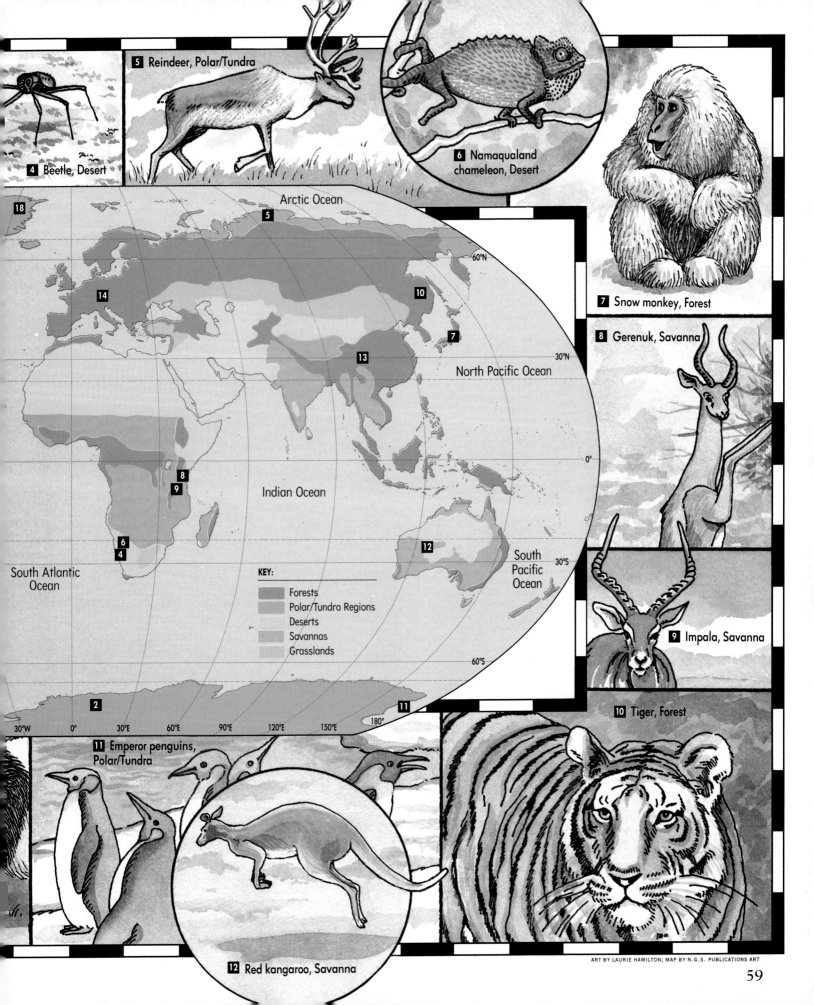

5 Reindeer, Polar/Tundra

4 Beetle, Desert

6 Namaqualand chameleon, Desert

7 Snow monkey, Forest

8 Gerenuk, Savanna

9 Impala, Savanna

10 Tiger, Forest

11 Emperor penguins, Polar/Tundra

12 Red kangaroo, Savanna

Arctic Ocean

60°N

30°N

North Pacific Ocean

Indian Ocean

0°

South Atlantic Ocean

30°S

South Pacific Ocean

60°S

30°W　0°　30°E　60°E　90°E　120°E　150°E　180°

KEY:

Forests
Polar/Tundra Regions
Deserts
Savannas
Grasslands

ART BY LAURIE HAMILTON; MAP BY N.G.S. PUBLICATIONS ART

Home
In the Biome

You're about to go on a biome trek. That means you're going to visit five major biomes: forests, savannas, deserts, grasslands, and polar/tundra regions. Scientists identify biomes by the plants that grow in them and by their climates. Each biome can be divided into smaller units. The grasslands biome, for instance, includes steppes and prairies. On your trip, you'll see more than landscapes. You'll meet animals that thrive in each place.

Why not start your adventure in the forest biome. Forests cover much of the earth's land. Because they get plenty of rain, trees are their main plants—in all shapes and sizes. Some forests have trees that shed leaves once a year. Others, such as rain forests, are filled with trees that stay green all year. Hundreds of kinds of trees grow in a rain forest. Many reach the height of a 20-story building.

At the edge of a forest, you'll often find a savanna. A savanna receives less rain than a forest does, so you'll see fewer trees. Where you don't see trees, you'll see stretches of grass dotted with shrubs. You'll discover many different grasses, including one kind that grows 16 feet tall.

Before you step into the desert biome, you'll want to fill your canteen. Only about ten inches of rain—or less—falls in a desert in a year. Desert plants and animals live on small amounts of water. How? Some plants store water in their stems or leaves. Some animals drink droplets of fog.

You'll find that a grasslands biome has more extreme temperature changes from season to season than the other biomes do. Its rainfall is only slightly greater than a desert's. For those reasons, trees are rare. Tough grasses survive best. In the driest areas, some grasses have roots that grow 20 feet down to reach water.

At last, bundle up and enter the polar/tundra biome. In tundra regions, scattered grasses, shrubs, and flowers grow in the summer. In winter, snow covers the ground. Polar regions are ice-covered in every season.

To find out which biome is home to which creatures in this chapter, match the color bars on the following pages with the colors on the map on pages 58–59.

PETER R. GIMBEL

ANIMALS ANIMALS/MICHAEL FOGDEN

ANIMALS ANIMALS/ZIG LESZCZYNSKI

▲ Meet the world's slowest land mammal, the three-toed sloth. A sloth spends most of its time hanging from tree branches. Its legs aren't made for walking. When it does climb to the ground, it pulls itself along with its front claws. Sloths live in rain forests in Central and South America.

◀ What's wet and wild? A rain forest such as this one in Peru, in South America. On earth, you'll find several natural communities called biomes. Each has its own climate, and its own plants and animals. Rain forests are part of the forest biome. In a rain forest, it may rain almost every day. The temperature stays near 80°F. Thousands of kinds of plants and wildlife thrive in the steamy climate.

▲ "Boo!" A Trinidad tree frog peers from its rain forest perch. It lives only in Trinidad, an island nation off the northeast coast of South America. The frog is about three inches long. Pads at the ends of its toes help it cling to slippery branches.

▶ It's a North Pole parade. In the polar/tundra biome, these arctic foxes are padding behind the polar bear for a good reason. The bear may be headed for a kill it made earlier, perhaps a seal. After the bear dines on the seal, the foxes will eat any leftovers. As the bear and foxes trudge along, they are protected from cold winds by thick fur coats. Why doesn't the bear grab a fox for a snack? If a ready-caught meal weren't nearby, it might try to.

▶ Adélie (uh-DAY-lee) penguins leap onto an icy shore in Antarctica. Like all other penguins, Adélies have wings that are too small for flying. But penguins are the world's fastest water birds. They swim through polar seas, eating tiny creatures called krill. If a seal or other enemy threatens, most of the birds race to shore at such high speed that they easily pop up to land—and to safety.

◀ Calm and cool, a Weddell seal rests on the ice near the South Pole. An air-breathing animal, it came up through a hole it kept open in the ice. There it is safe from its enemies. When the seal dives to catch fish, however, it must avoid killer whales and leopard seals. The Weddell seal usually outswims them. Scientists think it may dive deeper and hold its breath longer than any other seal—as long as an hour.

ANTHONY BANNISTER (ABOVE AND RIGHT)

KARL H. SWITAK

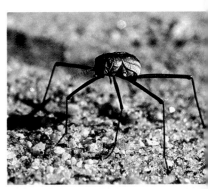

Fog drifts over Africa's Namib Desert. Part of the desert biome, the Namib is one of the world's driest places. But fog and rare rains provide enough moisture to keep many kinds of plants and animals alive. One kind of beetle stands with its head down and its back to the wind. Drops of fog cover its back and trickle into its mouth. One kind of plant lives on rainwater that collects underground.

A chameleon (kuh-MEEL-yun), a kind of lizard, inflates its body to scare away an enemy—perhaps a snake. Most chameleons live in forests. One kind, the Namaqualand (nah-muh-kwuh-LAND) chameleon, at left, lives in the Namib. A chameleon moves its eyes separately, so it can look backward and forward at once to seek prey. Then it catches insects with its long tongue. For water, it licks moisture from leaves, or waits for fog to seep through its skin.

A different kind of "dune buggy," a desert beetle picks its way across the Namib. Stilt-like legs keep the beetle's body away from the desert's burning sand. At midday, when the desert is hottest, some beetles burrow a few inches into the sand to a cooler spot.

NATIONAL GEOGRAPHIC PHOTOGRAPHER JOSEPH J. SCHERSCHEL

▶ Wildebeests (WILL-duh-beests) graze on Africa's Serengeti Plain, in the savanna biome. Wildebeests are a kind of antelope. In rainy seasons, they eat grass in one area. In dry seasons, when the grass becomes scarce there, they go hundreds of miles to find food.

▼ It's snack time for the gerenuk (GER-uh-nook). The animal, also an antelope, lives in eastern Africa. To eat high leaves, it stands on its hind legs and balances against a bush. Some scientists think that gerenuks get enough moisture from leaves so that they never have to drink water.

INDEX STOCK INT'L/PRISCILLA CONNELL

▶ Alert to danger, impalas (im-PAL-uhz) prepare to scatter. Impalas, another kind of antelope, live in parts of southeastern Africa. If a herd senses danger, its members race off in all directions, leaping over tall grasses and bushes. In a savanna version of leapfrog, they even jump over each other. The motion confuses a predator. As the impalas vanish, they often leave a hungry lion behind.

© GUNTER ZIESLER/PETER ARNOLD, INC.

◀ *You can see for miles across this prairie in North America. Part of the grassland biome, it covers areas of the midwestern United States and three Canadian provinces. Here, in Iowa, spring flowers called blazing stars carpet the ground. If you could explore the entire prairie, you'd see dozens of kinds of wildflowers and grasses. You'd see animals from blackbirds to bison.*

◀ *"Watch out!" Sensing danger, a bison mother bawls a warning as she stands guard over her calf. You may know these animals by another name: American buffaloes. They are the heaviest native land animals in North America. Bison feed on grass—plenty of it. Males may grow to a height of six and a half feet at the shoulder. They may weigh a ton or more. As many as 60 million bison once roamed North America. Gradually, people killed most of them off. By 1889, fewer than 600 remained in the wild. Today, laws protect bison. Thousands now graze in parks and preserves.*

▲ *Boom! No, it isn't a thunderclap. It's the mating call of a male Attwater's prairie-chicken. To attract a female, the male draws air into pouches in his neck. Then he noisily deflates them. About 1,100 of these prairie-chickens survive in Texas grasslands.*

Wow, What Weather!

Lightning streaks across the sky. Thunder booms in the distance. Quick! Run for shelter! You're in for a downpour. Not every place has this kind of weather. Different kinds of weather are found in different places. In some places, it often rains each summer and snows each winter. In other places, it rarely rains and never snows.

Weather is the condition of the atmosphere at a particular place during a brief period of time. The condition may be snowy, rainy, or sunny. The brief period of time may be a few minutes or a few hours. The average pattern of weather that occurs in a place year after year is called its climate. When you say a place has a certain climate, that means it has about the same kinds of changes in the weather at about the same times each year. If you live in or near Washington, D. C., you're close to the northern limits of the subtropical moist climate. Each year, you expect the summers to be warm to hot, with moderate rainfall. You expect the winters to be cool, with light snowfall. If you live in parts of North Africa, you're used to a desert climate. You plan on little rainfall.

Different places have different climates. Why? Latitude plays a big part. If you live on or near the Equator, you get direct rays from the sun all year. In most cases, the climate is tropical. The weather is always warm. As you move away from the Equator and toward the Poles, you leave the sun's direct rays. Gradually, average temperatures grow cooler. In general, the less direct the rays are at a place, the cooler its climate is for parts of the year.

Elevation also helps affect climate. If you live at the base of the African mountain Kilimanjaro, your climate promises a full year of warm weather. But if you could live on the *top* of the mountain, you'd have snowy weather all year. Distance from the water may make a difference in climate, too. Ocean currents from polar regions cool some coastlines in the summer. Currents from the Equator bring warm temperatures to other coastlines in the winter.

Wherever you live, you have to adapt to your climate, just as the girl on the next page has had to adapt to hers.

◀ *Zap! Lightning strikes near Kitt Peak National Observatory, in Arizona. To capture several bolts in one picture, the photographer left his camera shutter open longer than usual. Thunderstorms are common in most climates. At any moment, about 1,800 such storms are rumbling throughout the world. Every second, about a hundred bolts flash between clouds and the ground. Each one heats the air to 54,000°F. That's hotter than the sun's surface.*

STEVE MCCURRY

▲ *Leaf-covered water floods this girl's yard on the island of Java, in Indonesia. Indonesia's climate is hot and steamy. In your climate, you might expect snow during the winter. In Indonesia, people expect winter winds called monsoons. The winds carry rain that drenches Java and nearby islands. The rain causes floods, but helps the crops.*

GARY LADD

© WILLIAM E. TOWNSEND, JR./PHOTO RESEARCHERS

▲ Watch your step! It's a half-mile drop to the bottom of Waimea (wy-MAY-uh) Canyon, on the Hawaiian island Kauai (kuh-WAH-ee). Waimea Canyon gets an average of 45 inches of rain a year. About ten miles away, Mount Waialeale (wy-ahl-ay-AHL-ay) receives about ten times more. Clouds blowing in from the ocean drop most of their moisture on Waialeale. By the time the clouds reach Waimea Canyon, they can release only light rains.

▶ It's raining . . . it's pouring . . . it's Mount Waialeale. Although the mountain is just a short distance from Waimea Canyon, its climate is very different. An average of 460 inches of rain falls here each year. That makes Mount Waialeale the wettest spot on land. Breezes blowing from the ocean carry clouds filled with moisture. The clouds ascend the mountain and cool down. The cooling causes them to lose their moisture as rain. If the sun shines while it rains, Hawaiians call the soft showers "liquid sunshine."

PAUL CHESLEY/PHOTOGRAPHERS ASPEN

GEO-QUIZ!

Can you name the driest desert on earth?

It's the Atacama (at-uh-KAHM-uh) Desert, in Chile, in South America. The desert averages three inches of rain a year. Some parts are so dry that it would be impossible to measure their rainfall. In some desert towns the roofs are full of holes. People see no need to re-pair them. The tamarugo (TAM-uh-ROO-go) tree grows only in the Atacama. Its roots reach deep underground for water.

LAURIE HAMILTON

Strrrrretch! In Dallas, Texas, a window washer cleans the glass side of a tall hotel. In the glass you can see reflections of other buildings. Since 1841, Dallas has grown from one log cabin beside the Trinity River into one of the largest cities in the United States.

Meeting People

INTRODUCTION

4

"The Big D." That's what some people call this city. You may know it better as Dallas, Texas. As you walk along the streets, you look skyward and see a window washer cleaning the glass side of a tall hotel. In the glass, you see reflections of other big buildings that line the streets of downtown Dallas. Would you be surprised to learn that Dallas started as a single log cabin beside the Trinity River? Today nearly two million people live in the city and its suburbs. The discovery of oil near Dallas boosted its growth.

If you live in Dallas, you may wear cowboy boots, eat barbecued ribs, and speak English with a Texas accent. But if you're a Lapp and you live in Norway, in northern Europe, as the boy on page 91 does, you may wear deerskin boots, eat reindeer meat, and speak a language called Lappish. What if you live in Mali (MAH-lee), in West Africa? You might live in a house like those on page 86. You might wear no shoes at all, eat bread made from a grain called millet, and speak Bambara. Why are people so different? Location provides some answers. People often eat food they find near their homes. They usually wear clothes that suit their climate.

Culture provides other answers. A culture is the traditional way of life that a group of people passes from one generation to another. It may take hundreds of years for a culture to develop. What traditions make up culture in the United States? Here are a few: eating hamburgers and apple pie, celebrating Independence Day on July 4, and wearing blue jeans. These are practices begun years ago and passed from generation to generation.

Your geo-whiz journey has taken you all over the world. Now get ready to travel again. This time, you'll look at different cultures. In them, you'll meet new people. You'll speak their languages and taste their foods. You'll visit their homes and join their celebrations. As you go, be prepared for fun: that's one thing you'll find in any culture.

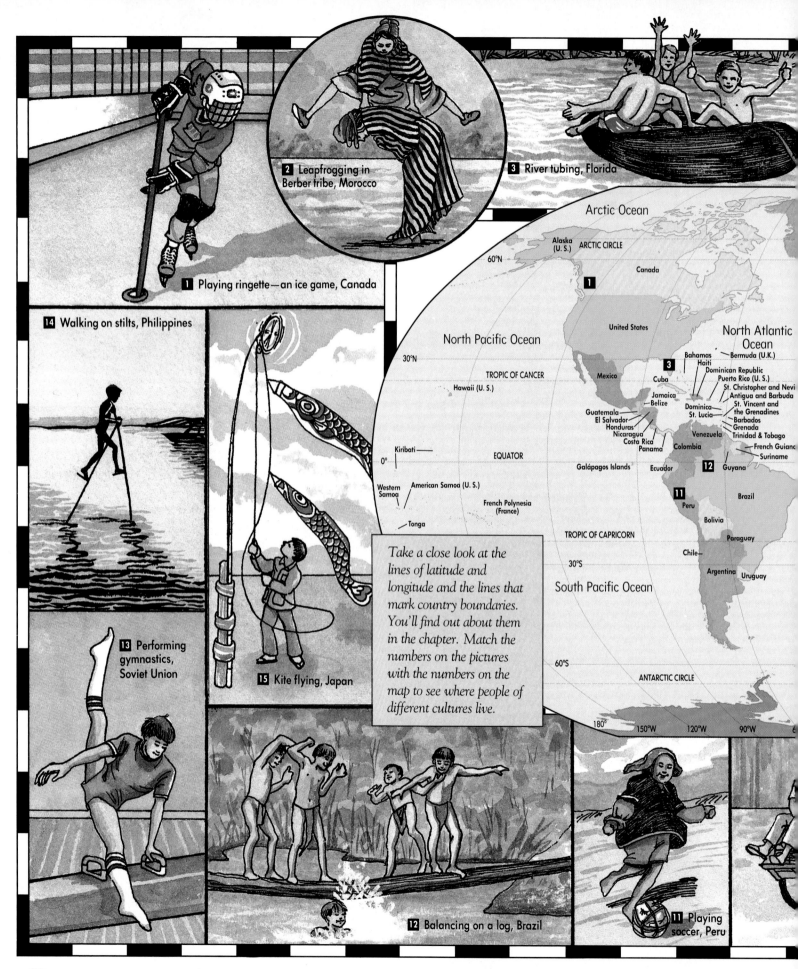

2 Leapfrogging in Berber tribe, Morocco

3 River tubing, Florida

1 Playing ringette—an ice game, Canada

14 Walking on stilts, Philippines

13 Performing gymnastics, Soviet Union

15 Kite flying, Japan

12 Balancing on a log, Brazil

11 Playing soccer, Peru

Take a close look at the lines of latitude and longitude and the lines that mark country boundaries. You'll find out about them in the chapter. Match the numbers on the pictures with the numbers on the map to see where people of different cultures live.

Arctic Ocean

Alaska (U. S.)   ARCTIC CIRCLE

60°N

Canada

1

North Pacific Ocean

United States

North Atlantic Ocean

30°N

TROPIC OF CANCER

Mexico

Hawaii (U. S.)

Bahamas   Bermuda (U.K.)
Haiti
Dominican Republic
Puerto Rico (U. S.)
St. Christopher and Nevi
Antigua and Barbuda
St. Vincent and
the Grenadines
Barbados
Grenada
Trinidad & Tobago

3

Cuba

Jamaica
Belize

Guatemala
El Salvador
Honduras
Nicaragua
Costa Rica
Panama

Dominica
St. Lucia

Venezuela

Colombia

French Guiana
Suriname

Kiribati

EQUATOR

Galápagos Islands

Ecuador

12

Guyana

0°

Western Samoa

American Samoa (U. S.)

French Polynesia (France)

11

Peru

Brazil

Tonga

Bolivia

TROPIC OF CAPRICORN

Chile

Paraguay

30°S

South Pacific Ocean

Argentina   Uruguay

60°S

ANTARCTIC CIRCLE

180°   150°W   120°W   90°W

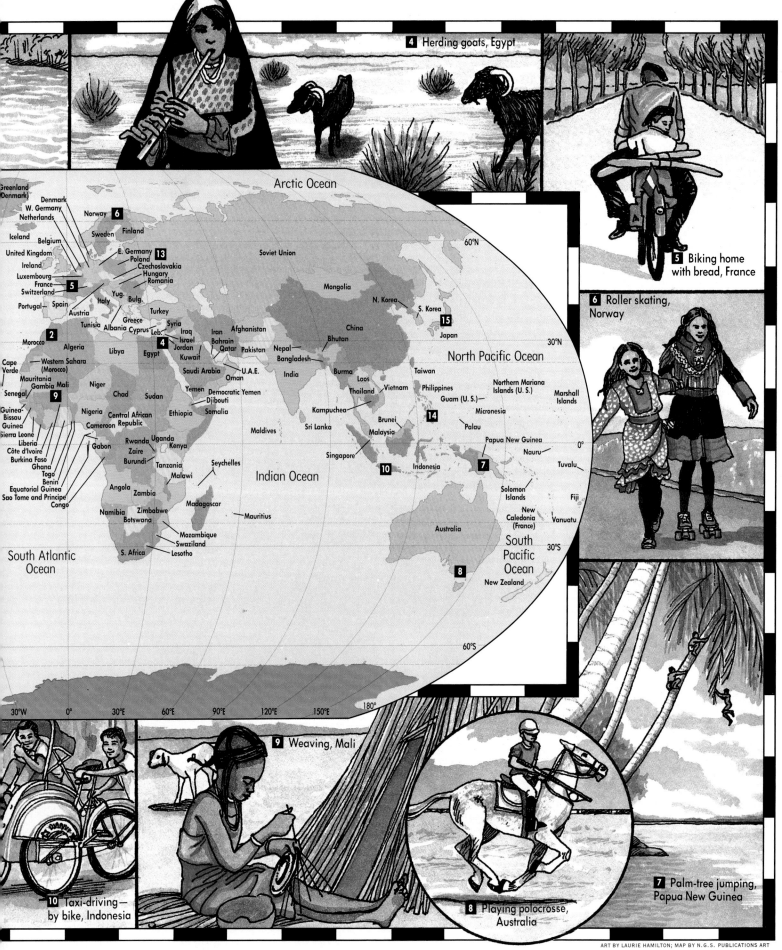

4 Herding goats, Egypt

5 Biking home with bread, France

6 Roller skating, Norway

7 Palm-tree jumping, Papua New Guinea

8 Playing polocrosse, Australia

9 Weaving, Mali

10 Taxi-driving—by bike, Indonesia

Arctic Ocean

Greenland (Denmark)
Denmark
W. Germany
Netherlands
Iceland
Belgium
United Kingdom
Ireland
Luxembourg
France **5**
Switzerland
Portugal
Spain
Italy
Austria
Tunisia
Morocco **2**
Algeria
Cape Verde
Western Sahara (Morocco)
Mauritania
Gambia Mali
Senegal
Guinea-Bissau
Guinea
Sierra Leone
Liberia
Côte d'Ivoire
Burkina Faso
Ghana
Togo
Benin
Equatorial Guinea
Sao Tome and Principe
Congo
Gabon
Cameroon
Nigeria
Niger
Chad
Central African Republic
Libya
Egypt **4**
Sudan
Ethiopia
Somalia

Norway **6**
Sweden
Finland
E. Germany
Poland **13**
Czechoslovakia
Hungary
Romania
Yug.
Bulg.
Albania
Greece
Cyprus
Turkey
Leb.
Syria
Iraq
Israel
Jordan
Kuwait
Saudi Arabia
Bahrain
Qatar
U.A.E.
Oman
Yemen
Democratic Yemen
Djibouti

9

Soviet Union

Mongolia

Iran
Afghanistan
Pakistan
Nepal
Bangladesh
India
Bhutan
China
Burma
Laos
Thailand
Vietnam
Kampuchea
Sri Lanka
Maldives

N. Korea
S. Korea **15**
Japan

North Pacific Ocean

Taiwan
Philippines
Guam (U. S.)
Northern Mariana Islands (U. S.)
Marshall Islands
Micronesia
Palau
Brunei **14**
Malaysia
Singapore
Indonesia **10**
Papua New Guinea **7**
Nauru
Tuvalu
Solomon Islands
Fiji
New Caledonia (France)
Vanuatu

Rwanda
Zaire
Burundi
Uganda
Kenya
Tanzania
Malawi
Angola
Zambia
Zimbabwe
Namibia
Botswana
Mozambique
Swaziland
Lesotho
S. Africa

Seychelles
Madagascar
Mauritius

Indian Ocean

Australia **8**

New Zealand

South Pacific Ocean

South Atlantic Ocean

60°N
30°N
0°
30°S
60°S

30°W 0° 30°E 60°E 90°E 120°E 150°E 180°

ART BY LAURIE HAMILTON; MAP BY N.G.S. PUBLICATIONS ART

73

People On the Move

D o you remember the nursery rhyme about the old woman who lived in a shoe? She had so many children she didn't know what to do. Like the population of the old woman's shoe, the population of the earth keeps growing.

On the day you were born, about 350,000 other people were born. Most have a chance to live longer than people did many years ago. Since the 1700s, scientists have learned how to cure many diseases and how to stop others from spreading. Agriculture experts have found ways to grow more food. With better health and more to eat, people are living longer. The world population is growing larger and larger. From 1930 to 1975, it doubled. Experts think that the next doubling will take less time.

In this book, you have seen hot and cold deserts, steep mountains, and huge fields of ice. Looking at them, you may have thought, "That's a nice place to visit, but I wouldn't want to live there." Most people would agree with you. People usually settle on land that meets their needs. Farmers look for water and fertile soil where crops can grow. Builders look for stretches of firm land where they can put up houses and office buildings. Shippers and merchants settle near waterfronts. How much of the earth's land do people find fit for living? Here's a surprise: Only about ten percent of the land is populated.

You'll find much of that population in cities. So many people live in cities that some cities have bigger populations than some countries do. For example, in 1987, Mexico City had about 20 million residents—that's four times as many as the entire country of Norway had.

Whether people live in cities or in the countryside, they must be able to travel from place to place. For thousands of years, people could travel only by land or by water. On land, they could go only as fast as they could walk or run, or an animal could pull or carry them. On water, they could move only as fast as they could row or sail. Today, superpowered vehicles help them get where they want to go in a hurry. As you turn the pages, you'll see some of the fastest ways to get from place to place.

▲ Who needs sidewalks? Pedestrians compete with drivers for space on the narrow streets of Taipei (TYE-PAY). This city of about two and a half million people is the capital of Taiwan (TYE-WAHN), an island off the coast of the People's Republic of China. In 1949, more than two million Chinese who disagreed with their new Communist government moved to Taiwan and started their own government. Many of them settled in Taipei. A scene like this is not unusual there and in other East Asian cities. More people live in Asia than anywhere else in the world.

◀ The tallest building in the world, the Sears Tower, rises 1,454 feet above Chicago, Illinois. More than 25,000 people—office workers and visitors—enter the building every weekday. That's more than the population of many towns in Illinois.

▲ Elevated expressways crisscross in Miami, Florida. The city's warm weather annually attracts millions of visitors and many new residents. As the population grows, cars crowd the roads. Thanks to expressways, traffic can move quickly. Such roads have no traffic signals or intersections, and many have six or more lanes.

GEO-QUIZ!

What term describes the time of day when the most traffic moves along city streets?

The term is "rush hour." In the United States, rush hour usually takes place when offices open and close, around nine in the morning and five in the afternoon. From the sound of the term, you might imagine people rushing to work and rushing home again. But in many cities, people can't rush during rush hour. So many cars crowd the streets that people sometimes sit for hours in bumper-to-bumper traffic. Some people who study the origin of words think the term "rush hour" came into use in the late 1800s, when there were fewer people, and it was easier to rush from place to place.

LAURIE HAMILTON

◀ Is it faster than a speeding bullet? Not quite, but with a top speed of 130 miles an hour, Japan's "bullet train" is one of the world's fastest trains. In about three hours, it zips 343 miles between Tokyo and Osaka. Fast as it is, the train can't beat France's TGV, which hits 170 miles an hour. TGV stands for Très Grande Vitesse, which means "very high speed."

NATIONAL GEOGRAPHIC PHOTOGRAPHER DEAN CONGER

▲ Up, up, and away! It's 1969, and the supersonic jet Concorde lifts off on a test flight from Toulouse (to-LOOZ), in France. The Concorde whizzes through the sky at 1,340 miles an hour—twice the speed of sound. This is the fastest way for the public to travel. The Concorde flies between France or England and the United States in only three and a half hours. That's half the time of a regular jet.

Lines
And Limits

I f you enjoy sports, you already know about certain kinds of boundaries. You have probably seen the lines that divide zones on a tennis court or a football field. Now make a stop in China and visit the Great Wall (right). You'll never see a boundary like this on a playing field. What makes the Great Wall so great? It runs more than 1,500 miles across what was once China's northern border.

Boundaries mark the place where one region, such as a country, ends and another region begins. Often the area on one side of a boundary looks just like the area on the other side. People, often through warfare, decide where boundaries go. Sometimes a natural feature such as a mountain range or a river becomes a boundary. The St. Lawrence River forms part of the boundary between the United States and Canada. Sometimes a boundary follows an imaginary line. Then people may put up buildings or fences to mark the boundary. A country surrounded by water, such as Australia, does not share a boundary with any other country. But the Soviet Union, in Europe and Asia, shares boundaries with 12 other countries.

Today people have divided most of the land on earth into countries. Boundaries mark the divisions. People have created boundaries in the ocean and in the air, too. What's next? People may establish boundaries in space.

▶ *Sightseers stroll along the Great Wall of China. Long ago, Chinese rulers decided to build a wall to protect the country's northern border against invaders. Using stones and bricks, workers began construction. By the 1600s, the wall stretched across China. Its length: more than 1,500 miles.*

▶ Boundaries don't stop these camel riders, who are called Tuareg (TWAH-regg) nomads. For centuries, Tuaregs have roamed North African deserts, searching for food and water for their cattle and other livestock. They also carry salt by caravan from one part of Africa to another. Recently, some African governments have set up checkpoints along country borders to control travel and to collect taxes. For the Tuaregs, crossing the borders is more complicated than it once was.

▶ One look, and you'll know why this area is called the Thousand Islands region. This stretch of the St. Lawrence River forms part of the boundary between the United States and Canada. The river is more than a boundary. It's a major shipping route. The St. Lawrence flows into North America's Great Lakes. The river and lakes combined make up the largest inland navigation system on the continent.

◀ To your right, Canada. To your left, the United States. As you walk this path through a forest in the Rocky Mountains, you can see the line where the two countries meet. An international commission keeps the 20-foot-wide trail cleared of trees. This section of the path runs between the state of Montana, in the United States, and the Canadian province of Alberta.

SOVIET UNION

Alaska

GEO-QUIZ!

The lines that divide the United States into states have always been the same. True or False?

False. Through the years, the states' boundary lines have been set—or changed—by treaties, charters, purchases, and acts of Congress. Today, the U.S. consists of 50 states, 48 of which are contiguous. That means the border of each state touches the border of at least one other state. Hawaii and Alaska are the two detached states. Of course, you won't see boundary lines on the land. The lines are drawn on maps. Usually signs or natural features mark the actual boundaries. One boundary between Alaska and Canada is marked by 233 signs. Hawaii doesn't need markers. It doesn't touch the border of any other state or country. To find out more about boundaries, try the quiz at right. Use the map as a guide. Check your answers in the column at far right.

LAURIE HAMILTON

1 Where can you stand in four states at once?

2 Which foreign country is closest to the United States without touching it?

3 Which states have only straight-line boundaries?

4 Which state has no straight-line boundaries?

7 If you traveled due south from Detroit, Michigan, in the United States, which foreign country would you reach first?

5 Which state shares a boundary with only one other state?

6 Does Virginia or West Virginia extend farther west?

Hawaii

80

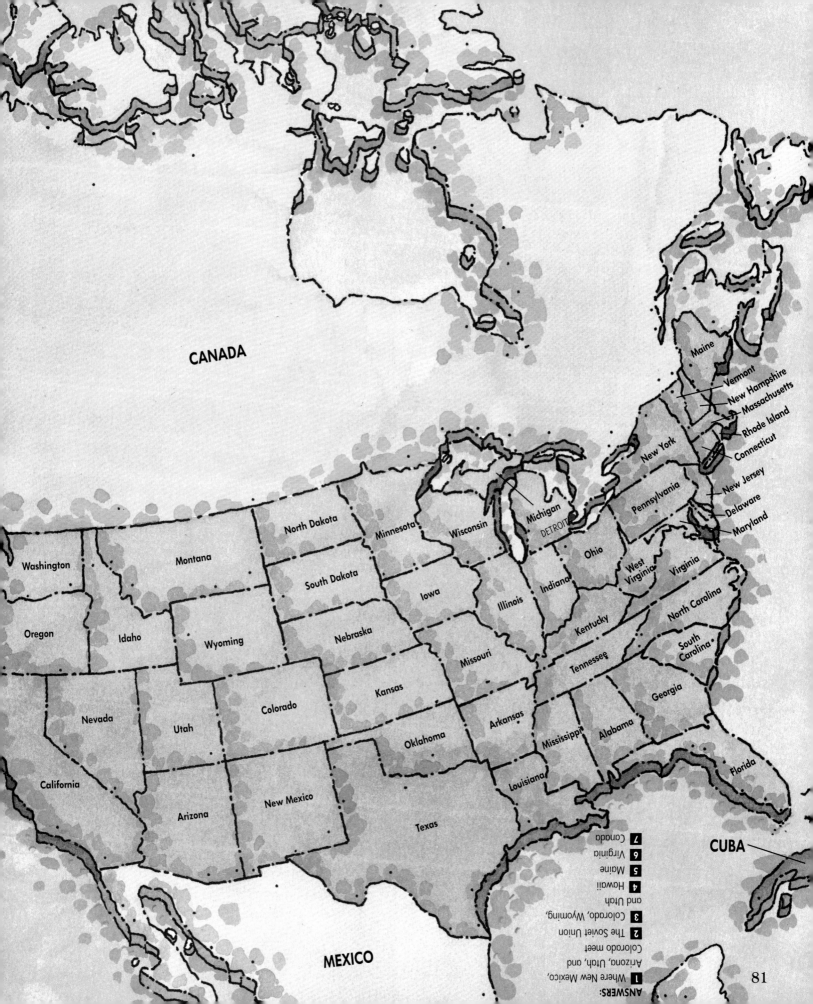

CANADA

Washington
Oregon
Idaho
Montana
North Dakota
Minnesota
Wisconsin
Michigan
DETROIT

Nevada
Utah
Wyoming
South Dakota
Iowa
Illinois
Indiana
Ohio
Pennsylvania
New York

California
Arizona
New Mexico
Colorado
Kansas
Nebraska
Missouri
Kentucky
West Virginia
Virginia
North Carolina

Oklahoma
Arkansas
Tennessee
Mississippi
Alabama
Georgia
South Carolina

Texas
Louisiana
Florida

Maine
Vermont
New Hampshire
Massachusetts
Rhode Island
Connecticut
New Jersey
Delaware
Maryland

MEXICO

CUBA

ANSWERS:

1 Where New Mexico, Arizona, Utah, and Colorado meet
2 The Soviet Union
3 Colorado, Wyoming, and Utah
4 Hawaii
5 Maine
6 Virginia
7 Canada

81

Where – And When

You are on your way to Hammerfest, in Norway (right). How will you find it? Someone might tell you to go to a point that is 72 degrees north latitude and 24 degrees east longitude. What on earth does that mean? If that person had said, "Turn right after the traffic light," or "Go ten miles past the red barn," it might make more sense. You can *see* a traffic light or a barn. But you cannot see lines of latitude or longitude. Scientists created them to divide the earth, and they appear only on globes and maps. You can use the lines to determine the exact location of places on earth.

Lines of latitude circle the earth in an east-west direction. Lines of longitude run in a north-south direction. On a map, the lines cross each other in a pattern called a grid. Since a single line of longitude and a single line of latitude cross at just one spot, you can use the grid to pinpoint any place on earth.

Now that you know how to find a place, can you figure out what time it is there? The time of any place depends on its longitude. Look at the chapter map. You'll see 12 lines of longitude. Each represents two hours. Normally, if you start at 0° longitude and travel east, you'll *gain* two hours at each line. If you travel west from 0°, you'll *lose* two hours at each line. So when it's 6 a.m. at 0° longitude, where is it noon? Answer: at 90° east longitude.

▶ *At Hammerfest, in northern Norway, it's close to midnight. Why is it so light? On its orbit, the earth is tilted in relationship to the sun. For part of the year, far northern regions face the sun. Then, the polar region is light for 24 hours a day. For another part of the year, the north tilts away from the sun. During that time, the sun doesn't shine in the far north at all.*

▲ *What time is it? Ask this scientist at the United States Naval Observatory, in Washington, D. C. The observatory has more than 40 clocks that run on atomic energy. Their average time is correct to within one-billionth of a second. The time at any place on earth depends upon the longitude of that place. The observatory clocks tell official times at certain longitudes across the United States.*

GEO-QUIZ!

Where could you play the first half of a football game in one year and the second half in the previous year?

At the international date line. That's a line on maps that runs from one pole to the other, mostly along the 180° longitude line. The date on the west side of the date line is a day ahead of the date on the east side. The line crosses ice or land only in the polar regions. There, on the west side of the line, you could play the first half of a football game on January 1. Then you could cross to the east side and play the second half on December 31 of the previous year!

Life's Styles

You're in Arizona, hiking into a rocky canyon 700 feet deep. Surprise! Suddenly, you see dozens of empty rooms inside a cave in the canyon wall. Indians built these rooms for homes about 750 years ago. To you, the structures might seem isolated and strange. That's because they look different from your own home. But the people who lived here felt comfortable in their cliff dwellings.

On the next few pages, you'll visit homes in the shapes of cones and domes. You'll visit a village where the houses are built in a circle. You'll visit a city that looks like a maze. You'll discover that people often build with the materials that are easiest to find. In parts of Africa where trees are scarce, many people use mud for their houses. People who live in or near forests often build homes of timber. Eskimos who live in the snowy, treeless north may carve blocks out of snow to build an igloo.

No matter where they live, people must shelter themselves from the weather. They must eat. And in most cases they must wear clothing to protect themselves from the environment. Depending on their culture, they prefer different styles of shelter, food, and clothing. For example, *you* might prefer to live in a house with just one family—yours. An Indian child in Brazil might prefer to live in a larger house with several families. *You* might enjoy an ice cream cone as a treat. An Alaskan Eskimo child might prefer a tasty bite of whipped seal oil with blueberries. *You* might wear a fancy dress or a jacket and tie for a special occasion. Some Indians in Brazil paint their faces and pierce their noses with reeds to dress for celebrations.

At the mention of whipped seal oil and pierced noses, did you say "Yuck!"? If you live in France, you might have said "Beeuurk!" instead. People everywhere use language to express their thoughts. Each language translates certain expressions and noises in a different way. Consider animal noises. In German, people say that gorillas *brüll*, not "roar." In Chinese, people describe a dog's bark as *wang wang*, not "woof woof." Read on to learn more about people and how they eat, dress, speak, and build their homes.

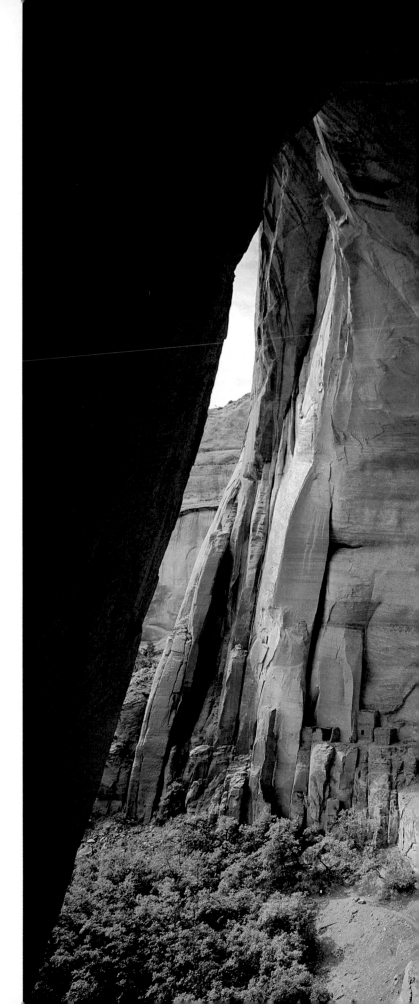

◀ *About 750 years ago, a small group of Indians settled in this Arizona cave. Scientists think they moved here because the cave offered protection from summer sun and winter snow. The Indians used rock, mud, and wood to build about 135 rooms along the cave wall. They lived in some rooms. In one, they held religious ceremonies. Others were storage rooms. To reach the ground below, they climbed down cliff walls beneath the dwellings, using indents they had chipped into the rock. Studies show that after only 50 years the Indians moved on, perhaps in search of better farmland. Centuries later, Navajo Indians who had moved to the area found the dwellings. The village is called Betatakin, which means "ledge house" in Navajo. You can see the houses at Navajo National Monument.*

▲ *An Eskimo crouches outside an igloo in Greenland. Igloos are made from blocks of hardened snow. Some Eskimos still use them, but only for shelter during winter travel.*

▲ *Living in a house like this, a fisherman doesn't have far to go to find work. This home was built on wooden stilts above Tonle Sap (tahn-lay SAP), in Kampuchea (kahm-POOCH-ee-ah). The Southeast Asian country was formerly called Cambodia.*

▲ A family in Cappadocia
(kap-uh-DOE-she-uh), a
region in Turkey, looks out
from the balcony of a cone-
shaped home. Thousands of
years ago a volcano erupted,
coating the earth with ash and
lava. These materials hardened
into solid rock. Slowly, erosion
shaped the rock into cones. For
more than a thousand years,
people have hollowed out the
cones, creating homes,
storerooms, and churches.
During Cappadocia's hot
summers, temperatures inside
the cones remain comfortable.

JAMES A. SUGAR

LOREN MCINTYRE

▲ Residents of this village in Zaire (zye-EAR), in Africa, take pride in their neat cottages. They call this section Beauty Road. The walls of the homes are built of bamboo stems packed with mud. The roofs are made of bamboo stems and leaves. In Zaire, many people raise fruits and vegetables. They often build their villages near main highways so they can sell the goods to passersby.

◄ Timbuktu! The name suggests a place so far away that it might not even exist. But Timbuktu does exist, in West Africa, and has for more than 900 years. The city sits on the southern edge of the Sahara in Mali. Its buildings of mud form a giant maze. In Timbuktu, months may go by without rain, and the walls remain sturdy. Rare rains may be so heavy that many walls must be repaired.

GEORG GERSTER

▲ At first glance, you might think this is a new kind of Ferris wheel. Glance again. It's a Krahó (krah-HO) Indian village, photographed from above. The Krahó Indians of Brazil arrange their villages in the shape of a wheel. The closed formation promotes a tight-knit community. Villagers hold meetings at the center.

GEO-QUIZ!

When were most of the world's castles built?

During the Middle Ages, which lasted from about the sixth century to the fifteenth. A castle was both home and fort. Powerful noblemen built castles big enough for their families, their armies of knights, and their knights' horses. They built castles all over Europe. How many? Thousands. Some people still call a castle home.

LAURIE HAMILTON

GEO-QUIZ!

Can you tell where a food comes from by its name?

Sometimes. Certain foods take the names of places where they are produced, or where they were invented. French toast is one example. It originated in France. Another French dish is quiche lorraine (keesh luh-RAIN)—a cheese pie that was first served in the French region of Lorraine. From Yorkshire, a county in England, comes a food called Yorkshire pudding. Some cheeses bear names of the cities or counties where they were created. Which cheese comes from Parma, a city in Italy? It's Parmesan. Which one comes from Monterey, a county in California? It's Monterey Jack. Study the foods at right. What places are they named for? Check the pictures and labels for clues. The answers appear in the box below.

ANSWERS:
1. Edam, in the Netherlands
2. Parts of Switzerland
3. Hamburg, in West Germany
4. Darjeeling, in India
5. Parts of Brazil
6. Frankfurt, in West Germany
7. Brussels, in Belgium
8. Dijon, in France
9. Brie, in France
10. Cheddar, in England

1 Edam Cheese

2 Swiss Cheese

10 Cheddar Cheese

3 Hamburger

88

4 Darjeeling Tea

5 Brazil Nuts

6 Frankfurter

GEO-QUIZ!

Where can you drop milk without spilling it?

In the town of Oymyakon (i'm-yuh-KONE), in the Soviet Union. It's the coldest town on earth. People there buy milk in frozen chunks. If they drop the milk while carrying it home, the chunks might break, but they won't spill, as a liquid would.

9 Brie Cheese

8 Dijon Mustard

7 Brussels Sprouts

LAURIE HAMILTON

QIMMIARANNGUAQARUMAVUNGA

There are languages in which you can express the thoughts of an entire sentence in a single word. True or False?

True. One such language is called Kalaallisut (kuh-LASS-lih-soot). It is spoken by Eskimos in West Greenland. To say something in English, people string several words together to form a sentence. To say something in Kalaallisut, people put *parts* of words together. Several parts can make up one long word. For example, an Eskimo child who wants a pet can say so in a single word: "Qimmiarannguaqarumavunga." An English-speaking child would need seven words to say the same thing: "I want to have a little puppy." What is the longest word in Kalaallisut? No one knows, since Kalaallisut speakers make up new words all the time. Here's one very long Kalaallisut word that Eskimo children might use around their birthdays: "Inuuissiornilersaarfigiartortariaqaraluarpakka." Its 12-word English translation is: "I really have to go and tell them about the birthday party."

LAURIE HAMILTON

GEORG GERSTER

► Even while she does her chores, an Egyptian girl wears bracelets, earrings, and a necklace. Perhaps twice a day, she fills jugs with water from a local well and carries them home. Because summers in Egypt are hot, she wears loose clothing to stay comfortable. On her head she had been wearing a scarf. It has slipped to her shoulders.

NICHOLAS DEVORE III/PHOTOGRAPHERS ASPEN

◄ Shells, beads, and coins are part of an ornate hairdo for this girl from Mali. Like many girls in the United States, she wears earrings in her pierced ears. If her family's income increases, more and more gold may be hammered onto the earrings until they are as big as cereal bowls. Some women of her tribe have earrings so big that they wear head straps to help support the heavy jewelry.

LYNN ABERCROMBIE

◄ To be at home on the range, every cowboy needs a hat like the one this boy in Montana wears. In the 1800s, cowboys wore similar hats on cattle roundups in the western United States. Some still do. Such hats shield them from rain, wind, and sun. The hats make good buckets, too. Some are so big that they're called ten-gallon hats.

▶ To attend a local craft fair in New Mexico, this Pueblo Indian girl has dressed up in an outfit like those her ancestors wore, complete with eagle, turkey, and parrot feathers. During the year, she may wear the costume on other special days. One, Feast Day, honors San Ildefonso, the saint her pueblo was named for. On that day, her tribe will perform age-old Pueblo dances. One dance portrays a victory over the Comanche Indians.

◀ This boy, from Norway, wears traditional clothing to do a traditional job: herding reindeer over grazing lands above the Arctic Circle. The boy belongs to a group called Lapps. For centuries, Lapps in Norway and nearby countries have herded reindeer. Heavy felt jackets provide warmth.

◀ On most days, this girl ties a black scarf around her head. Then she pins a striped blanket around her shoulders. She is a member of a Berber tribe that lives in Morocco, in North Africa. Today is a holiday. To dress up, she painted her face and tied red yarn with spangles around her scarf. When she is older, she may have a tattoo applied to her chin.

▼ This boy is from a tribe in Papua New Guinea (PAP-yuh-wuh new GIHN-ee), part of an island north of Australia. He is ready to sing and dance in a ceremony called a sing-sing. Sing-sings often celebrate good harvests. First, he had to stand very still while someone painted his face. Members of his village made the paints from clay and berries. Wearing paints, beads, and a feathered fur cap, the boy looks much as his ancestors did at their sing-sings generations before.

◀ No, she's not a doll. She's a real live girl, wearing chalk-white makeup and a shiny black wig. She's taking part in a ceremony in Japan. Her costume illustrates the way some Japanese have dressed for centuries. This garment is called a kimono. Today most Japanese wear kimonos only for special occasions.

▲ It's party time, and this Indian girl has just finished getting ready. She lives in Brazil's Amazon rain forest. Her mother or a friend painted her face with charcoal or with dye made from fruit. Feathers decorate her ears. In her pierced nose and chin she wears narrow reeds. Now she will attend a feast at a neighboring village.

Let the Good Times Roll!

You've reached your next stop: the desert in Saudi Arabia. You see people charging across the sand on camels. Spectators cheer and wave. Thousands have gathered to watch the annual King's Camel Race—and to have a good time.

Get ready! You're going to have a good time, too. You're about to watch a parade, a festival, and several dances. You'll see how people around the world have fun. You'll find out how their celebrations reflect their cultures. For instance, you'll watch dancers in Africa, Europe, and Asia as they do the same steps their ancestors did ages before. People have been kicking up their heels to dance for a long time. Prehistoric paintings show that people were dancing at least four thousand years ago.

One celebration is common in many cultures: the harvest festival. For centuries, farmers have given thanks for the food they have grown and harvested. Today farmers and nonfarmers alike still observe harvest holidays. In Africa, some groups perform harvest dances. In France, many winegrowers hold fairs to celebrate grape harvests. Did you dine on turkey last Thanksgiving? If so, you were celebrating North America's harvest.

Like the people on these pages, you probably celebrate other events each year—including your own birthday.

◀ *When this boy in Zaire does a war dance, it doesn't mean he's going to war. His dance symbolizes the past bravery of warriors in his tribe, the Intoré (an-tor-AY). African tribe members dance on many occasions. They may dance when someone is born or married, or when crops are planted or harvested. In this dance, people carry spears and shields and wear headdresses.*

▲ Teenage dance students in Thailand practice moves that dancers in their country have used for generations. Through the moves, the students learn to tell stories. The slightest hand gesture adds to the tale.

◀ Which camel is the fastest? Every year in Saudi Arabia, hundreds of people ride in the King's Camel Race. Each rider hopes his camel will speed across miles of desert to cross the finish line first. The winning rider receives money and prizes. The winning camel receives food and fame. Spectators include the king of Saudi Arabia. The race was started in 1975 by a king who wanted to keep alive the tradition of camel racing practiced by nomads.

ROBERT AZZI

▲ This Eskimo isn't really flying. At a whaling festival in Alaska, a circle of other Eskimos have tossed him sky-high off an animal-skin blanket. Eskimos usually toss each other to celebrate the arrival of spring, a religious holiday, or a successful hunt.

93

GEO-QUIZ!

What island nation celebrates the day it was settled by British convicts?

Australia—the only nation in the world that occupies an entire continent. In 1788, British prisons were overcrowded. The government sent about 700 convicts, a governor, and guards to Australia to start a colony. More convicts and other settlers followed, and many colonies were started. Today, Australia's population tops 15 million. Australians celebrate the first colonization each year on January 26—Australia Day.

LAURIE HAMILTON

94

◀ A roof makes a good resting place for two dancers— stilt dancers, that is. Stilt dancing is a tradition among African tribes, such as this one in Côte d'Ivoire (coat dee-vwahr). To prepare, dancers first cut wooden poles, sometimes to a length of ten feet. To the poles, they attach small platforms for standing. Last, they bind their legs to the stilts with cloth strips. Like acrobats, the dancers turn, jump, and kick on the stilts. They perform whenever they feel the urge to dance.
MICHAEL AND AUBINE KIRTLEY

▶ Happy New Year! Spectators line a main street of Pasadena, California, to enjoy a New Year's Day tradition: the Tournament of Roses Parade. Marching bands, high-stepping horses, and fancy floats wind their way through the city. On this float, the feathers for a parrot and the costume for a giant Aztec warrior are made from marigolds, carnations, and other flowers. For about 48 hours before the parade begins, workers decorate floats with flowers, bark, and seeds. In 1987, they used about 20 million flowers on 60 floats. Pasadena's New Year's parade began nearly 100 years ago as a local celebration. Today, millions of people all over the world watch it on television.

JOHN DOMINIS/WHEELER PICTURES

◀ Old customs live on in Yugoslavia, in Eastern Europe. During tourist season, dance groups in many towns, such as Čilipi (CHILL-lip-ee), shown here, perform centuries-old dances. In Yugoslavia, people once danced to ask their gods to heal the sick or to make crops grow. Today, they dance mostly for entertainment.

Lasting Impressions

So far on your geo-whiz journey, you've discovered how people adapt to their environments: how they dress, eat, and find shelter. Now you'll see how they change their environments. For ages, people have built bridges, dug tunnels, and put up buildings to suit their needs. In the process, they have made lasting impressions on the land.

You're about to take a look at many different structures. You'll drop by Easter Island, in the South Pacific Ocean, to see ancient statues of stone. Then you'll glance at New York City, to see modern high rises of concrete and steel. Which would be harder to build: a sleek skyscraper or a primitive monument? Before you answer, remember that today's builders use equipment such as bulldozers, power drills, cranes, and computers. Ancient builders often had only such things as handmade tools, ladders, and ropes.

Because those ancient workers used only handmade tools, their grand creations seem all the more remarkable. Consider the Great Pyramid of Egypt. The people who built it started with a 13-acre base and stacked up two million stone blocks to a single point more than 480 feet above the ground. About five thousand years old, the pyramid is one of the wonders of the ancient world. It still stands as an example of precise engineering.

Each skyscraper, statue, or city bears the mark of the society that built it. Take a look at the land around you. What kind of lasting impressions has your society left?

▶ *Huge paws are all that remain of a lion carved into a rock called Sigiriya (si-GURR-yuh), right, in Sri Lanka. Sigiriya means "lion rock." The paws sit on either side of a stairway leading up the rock. People carved the lion and the stairs about 1,500 years ago. Then they built a palace on top of the rock.*

▶ *Giant faces gaze across Easter Island, in the South Pacific Ocean. Scientists think that more than a thousand years ago, islanders using stone picks chipped statues out of the island's volcanic rock. Then they loaded the carvings onto log rollers and hauled them to their present sites, as far as ten miles away. The statues weigh 20 tons or more. To push them up, the islanders probably set their bases on stone slabs, then shoved rocks under them.*

◀ *The road to these palace ruins is a rocky one. The ruins cover three acres on the top of Sigiriya. An ancient king in what is now Sri Lanka wanted to live where enemies couldn't reach him. He chose the top of this rock—600 feet above the jungle. Workers carved stairs in the rock. Then they carried up stones, logs, and tiles to build the palace.*

▶ *Vikings designed and built this fort in Denmark about a thousand years ago. At the center of the circle, two streets crossed. They divided the circle into four sections. In each section, four buildings formed a rectangle. The efficient design, based on ancient Roman forts, allowed warriors to reach the walls quickly during invasions. The Vikings built other forts in Denmark using the same plan.*

▲ *Putting up pyramids like these at Giza (GEEZ-uh), in Egypt, was no easy feat. Five thousand years ago, complex machinery did not exist. Some scientists think that laborers used copper chisels and saws to cut blocks from stone cliffs. They dragged the blocks to the pyramid site and pushed the first row into place. Then they built earthen ramps and hauled up row after row of the blocks, perhaps over 20 years' time.*

◀ *A helicopter cruises over Hoover Dam, in Black Canyon, on the border between Nevada and Arizona. In 1931, workers began building the dam to control flooding of the Colorado River. First they dug huge tunnels through the canyon walls to carry the river away from the construction site. Then they hollowed out a foundation for the dam in the dry riverbed. It took them five years and nearly seven million tons of concrete to build the dam. That's enough concrete to pave a highway running across the United States from coast to coast. Rising 725 feet, Hoover Dam is one of the tallest concrete dams in the world.*

▶ *If you had stood on this spot in Brazil in the 1940s, you would have seen grasslands all around you. Today, you'd look up at these office buildings. You'd also see roads, apartment houses, and stores. How did the grasslands become a city? In 1956, Brazil's president began fulfilling a campaign promise to develop the country's interior. His first step was to build a new capital 600 miles from the old one at Rio de Janeiro. Within three years, workers had put up the city of Brasília, and thousands of government employees had moved into it.*

▲ Go! Thousands of runners speed across the Verrazano-Narrows Bridge at the start of the 1985 New York City Marathon. The bridge links two boroughs, or districts, of New York City: Staten Island and Brooklyn. Completed in 1965, it spans 4,260 feet. It is one of the longest bridges in the world. One expert calculated that the wires used for its cables would circle the globe 55 times. You'll find hundreds of bridges in New York. The city, which contains 5 boroughs, has the largest population of any city in the United States.

▲ New York, New York! When you think of the city, does Manhattan Island come to mind? Manhattan is New York's smallest borough, but it is one of the world's top business and cultural centers. Dozens of skyscrapers line the Hudson River. Nearly two million people live there, and another three million commute to work there each day.

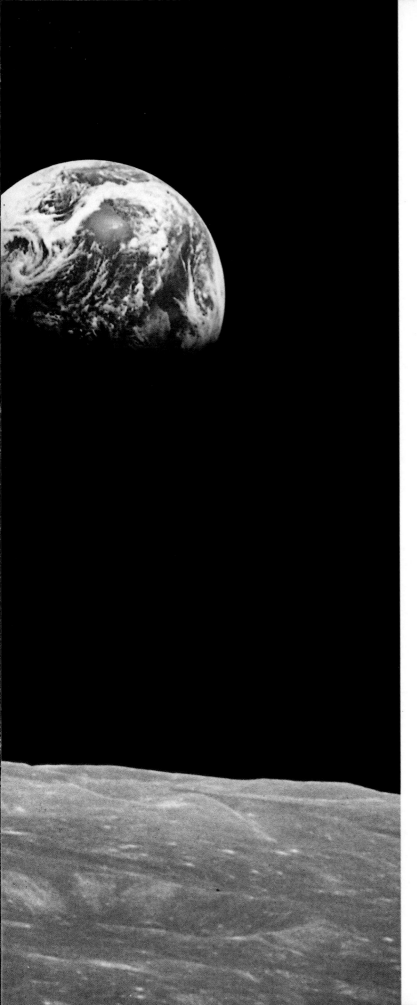

Welcome, Geo-Whiz!

5

Whew, what a trip! First you traveled all over the world, and now look where you are. You're at the moon. Over the moon's horizon, you see a bluish planet floating in space about 230,000 miles away. That big bluish ball is the earth. Does your planet look smaller than you thought it would?

On your geo-whiz journey, you've taken a closeup look at features on the earth. You've stood on high land and on low land. You've visited the wettest spot on earth and the driest. You've seen the slowest land mammal in the world and some of the fastest ones. You've met people who live in isolated forests, and in crowded cities. You've seen many things that are *different* from each other. Now you're looking at earth from space. You can see that, despite their differences, all the features and creatures on earth have something in common. They share a single home.

The people on earth depend on each other. Imagine that you're getting ready to go to school. You get dressed, grab your school supplies, and jump on the school bus. Your jacket may have been made in New York, your shoes in Taiwan. The wood of your pencil may have come from Oregon, the graphite core from Mexico. The gasoline that fuels your school bus may have come from oil fields in Alaska or in Saudi Arabia. People everywhere depend on other people, in other places, for many of the things they use every day.

You've learned something about maps in this book. You've also learned that maps are only part of geography. Geography concerns the relationship between people and the land. It concerns efforts to use earth's resources wisely. It concerns people and their cultures and traditions. Speaking of traditions, did you know that people have been studying geography for thousands of years? Now you've learned enough geography to become a certified geo-whiz—and you may sign the certificate in this book. Congratulations! You're carrying on an old tradition.

FRANK BORMAN/NASA

Index

102

ADDITIONAL READING

Readers may want to check the *National Geographic Index* in a school or public library for related articles and to refer to the following books: Coburn, Doris, *A Spit is a Piece of Land: Landforms in the U.S.A.*, Julian Messner, 1978. Deguine, Jean-Claude, *Earth in Motion*, William Morrow, 1978. Gilbreath, Alice, *Ring of Fire*, Dillon Press, 1986. Jacobs, Francine, *The Red Sea*, William Morrow, 1978. Johnson, Sylvia A., *Animals of the Temperate Forests*, Lerner, 1976. Knowlton, Jack, *Maps & Globes*, Thomas Y. Crowell, 1985. Matthews, William H. III, *Geology Made Simple*, Doubleday, 1982. McClintock, Jack, and Helgren, David, *Everything is Somewhere*, William Morrow, 1986. Radlauer, Ruth, and Anderson, Henry, *Reefs*, Childrens Press, 1983. Redfern, Ron, *The Making of a Continent*, Times Books, 1983. Seddon, Tony, and Baily, Jill, *The Physical World*, Doubleday, 1987. Whitlock, Ralph, *Penguins*, Raintree Childrens Books, 1977.

THE COVER

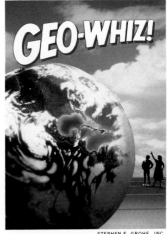

STEPHEN F. GROHE, INC.

If you zoomed in on earth from somewhere in space, you might see it as the children on the cover do. Of course, they aren't really in space and that isn't the earth they see. An artist and a photographer worked together to produce this image. A photocomposition, it's made of many elements. On your geo-journey you found out that earth, like this picture, is composed of many elements—from land and water to plants and people. By looking at those elements, you saw earth as these children see it—in a new, unusual way.

CONSULTANTS

Martha B. Sharma, National Cathedral School, Washington, D. C.; Peter B. Stifel, University of Maryland, *Chief Consultants*

Glenn O. Blough, LL.D., Emeritus Professor of Education, University of Maryland, *Educational Consultant*

Nicholas J. Long, Ph.D., *Consulting Psychologist*

Joan Winchester Myers, M.Ed. Reading, Alexandria City Schools, *Reading Consultant*

The Special Publications and School Services Division is also grateful to the individuals and institutions named or quoted in the text and to those cited here for their generous assistance:

John R. Apel, the Johns Hopkins University; James D. Belville, NOAA/National Weather Service; Barry C. Bishop, Timothy J. Carter, Harm de Blij, Alice T. M. Rechlin, Cathy Riggs-Salter, N.G.S.; Richard G. Boehm, Southwest Texas State University, San Marcos; Stephen Cairns, James Mead, Smithsonian Institution; Valerie Chase, National Aquarium in Baltimore; David R. Criswell, University of California; A. Morris Decker, Conley McMullen, D. E. Petzold, University of Maryland; Jon C. Campbell, Robert W. Decker, Jane G. Ferrigno, John A. Kelmelis, Diane C. Schnabel, Donald Swanson, Richard S. Williams, Jr., U. S. Geological Survey; Jack Fischer, British Airways; Glenn Gossard, Glen Canyon NRA; Axel Graumann, National Climatic Data Center; Guy Guthridge, Winifred Reuning, National Science Foundation; Roderick Hutchinson, Yellowstone National Park; Thomas Jenssen, Virginia Polytechnic Institute; Richard Libengood, Grand Canyon National Park; Laura Martin, Cleveland State University.

William H. Matthews III, Beaumont, Texas; Janet McClafferty, American Demographics; Roy McDiarmid, U. S. Fish and Wildlife Service; Arthur N. Palmer, SUNY at Oneonta; George Pararas-Cararyannis, International Tsunami Information Center; Larry W. Price, Portland, Oregon; Saul Price, National Weather Service; Jennifer Reeder, Embassy of Australia; Jerrold M. Sadock, University of Chicago; Rod Schipper, Kanab Resource Area-BLM; Steve Sheppard, Theodore J. Spilman, U. S. Department of Agriculture; Joan Smith, National Zoological Park; Mel Sunquist, Melrose, Florida; Sverrir Thorhallsson, National Energy Authority, Iceland; Thomas B. Thorson, University of Nebraska, Lincoln; Gary Vequist, Glacier Bay National Park; George E. Watson, St. Albans School, Washington, D. C.; Barbara J. Winston, Northeastern Illinois University; Thomas L. Wright, Hawaiian Volcano Observatory; William F. Zahner, University of New Mexico.

Composition for GEO-WHIZ! by the Typographic section of National Geographic Production Services, Pre-Press Division. Printed and bound by Holladay-Tyler Printing Corp., Rockville, Md. Film preparation by Catharine Cooke Studio, Inc., New York, N.Y. Color separations by Lincoln Graphics, Inc., Cherry Hill, N.J.; and NEC, Inc., Nashville, Tenn. Teacher's Guide printed by McCollum Press, Inc., Rockville, Md. Certificate printed by Peake Printers, Cheverly, Md.

Library of Congress CIP Data
Tejada, Susan Mondshein
Geo-Whiz! / by Susan Mondshein Tejada.
p.   cm. — (Books for world explorers)
Bibliography: p.
Includes index.
Summary: Text and pictures present startling and fascinating geographical, geological, and cultural facts from around the world.
ISBN 0-87044-662-2   ISBN O-87044-657-6 (pbk.)
1. Geography—Juvenile literature. [1. Geography. 2. Geology. 3.Manners and customs.] I. National Geographic Society (U. S.) II. Title. III. Series.
G133.T37   1988
910—dc19   87-28319
                                              CIP
                                              AC

GEO-WHIZ!

PUBLISHED BY
THE NATIONAL GEOGRAPHIC SOCIETY
WASHINGTON, D. C.
Gilbert M. Grosvenor, *President and Chairman of the Board*
Melvin M. Payne, Thomas W. McKnew, *Chairmen Emeritus*
Owen R. Anderson, *Executive Vice President*
Robert L. Breeden, *Senior Vice President,*
Publications and Educational Media

PREPARED BY THE SPECIAL PUBLICATIONS
AND SCHOOL SERVICES DIVISION
Donald J. Crump, *Director*
Philip B. Silcott, *Associate Director*
Bonnie S. Lawrence, *Assistant Director*

BOOKS FOR WORLD EXPLORERS
Pat Robbins, *Editor*
Ralph Gray, *Editor Emeritus*
Ursula Perrin Vosseler, *Art Director*
Margaret McKelway, *Associate Editor*
David P. Johnson, *Illustrations Editor*

STAFF FOR GEO-WHIZ!
M. Barbara Brownell, *Managing Editor*
Thomas B. Powell III, *Picture Editor*
Erin Taylor Monroney, *Assistant Picture Editor*
Sharon Davis, *Art Director*
Barbara L. Bricks, Lori Elizabeth Davie, *Researchers*
Martha C. Christian, Roger B. Hirschland, *Consulting Editors*
Patricia N. Holland, *Special Projects Editor*
Donna L. Hall, *Editorial Assistant*
Karen L. O'Brien, *Illustrations Assistant*
Janet A. Dustin, *Art Secretary*
John D. Garst, Jr., Virginia L. Baza, Isaac Ortiz,
Hildegard B. Groves, Gary M. Johnson, Joseph F. Ochlak,
Martin S. Walz, *Map Research and Production*
James T. Alton, *Editorial Intern*
Barbara Schwartz, *Geography Intern*

ENGRAVING, PRINTING, AND PRODUCT MANUFAC-
TURE: Robert W. Messer, *Manager;* George V. White, *Senior Assistant Manager;* Vincent P. Ryan, *Assistant Manager;* David V. Showers, *Production Manager;* Lewis R. Bassford, *Production Project Manager;* Gregory Storer, George J. Zeller, Jr., *Senior Assistant Production Managers;* Mark R. Dunlevy, *Film Archivist;* Timothy H. Ewing, *Production Assistant;* Carol R. Curtis, *Senior Production Staff Assistant*

STAFF ASSISTANTS: Aimée L. Clause, Betsy Ellison, Mary Elizabeth House, Kaylene F. Kahler, Sandra F. Lotterman, Eliza C. Morton, Nancy J. White

MARKET RESEARCH: Mark W. Brown, Joseph S. Fowler, Carrla L. Holmes, Marla Lewis, Donna R. Schoeller, Marsha Sussman, Judy Turnbull

INDEX: Lisa S. Jenkins